My Not
Recovery

Claire Hatwell

This book is dedicated to everyone who ever wondered if they had a drinking problem.

Believe me when I say there is hope, and if I can live and enjoy a life of sobriety with no regrets than anyone can.

Stay strong and be kind to yourselves xx

To my family, for always being there, for always loving me when I didn't always love myself, and for putting up with me even now.
I love you all more than words can say x

CHAPTER 1
MY NOT SO SECRET RECOVERY

The opening of a book about yourself isn't an easy thing to write. It's hard to define where the start should be because it means unpicking all the things that have gone before and reliving them. Revisiting the past isn't always a good thing, especially when it involves things you aren't so proud of, and yet mostly, however hard it may be, I find it really therapeutic in the long run. Writing helps me work things out about myself and eventually move on.

This book is ultimately the story of my addiction to alcohol and recovery to a life of sobriety. It sounds simple, but the process itself wasn't. Even admitting I was an alcoholic in the first place was near impossible, which made recovering from my problem a very difficult thing to do. I don't think the word 'alcoholic' helps, it's such a strong word and conjures up some pretty dark images in my mind at least. I wrote this book for a few reasons, one, because in the early days, weeks and months I devoured anything I could about addiction, recovery and mental health. In fact, I still do. I think it helps to realise that although we might face challenges, we aren't alone. There are so many people out there with different addictions that are also working to overcome them. By realising we aren't the only ones, it makes the mountain that we are trying to climb just that bit smaller and so by sharing how things were for me, I hope I can help someone else get through their challenge. The second reason is that writing actually helps me make sense of myself. As a huge over thinker I can get quite lost in my thoughts, the littlest thing can wind up into the biggest drama and I lose perspective. It makes me panic, although I am getting better, it has taken me years to get to where I am now. Writing however, seems to work well for me and once I start and the words begin to flow, it's very therapeutic for me. It helps me make sense of things and of myself in a way I wouldn't do otherwise, even for things that happened a long time ago.

I wouldn't say I have all the answers, but I have been there. I've tried recovery and failed. I tried again, (twice), and eventually I got there. I'm still here, and I hope that by sharing my story that I might give hope to others out there. I've loved writing from a young age, in fact as a child I had wanted to be a 'proper' writer, maybe a journalist, but we are talking before the internet made things a little easier, I was dissuaded. It seemed even then that it was assumed I was a bit fragile for an industry where people might have opinions on what I thought. I thought that forming a different career as I got older meant that my writing would disappear, for only me to see, but as often happens in life, one day it just seemed right to start actually letting people read my work. It was very hard, although it was probably harder for me to let people close to me read it than strangers and in some ways it still is, even now. It's one thing being judged by people who don't know you, but I was afraid of upsetting those close to me, and for a long time it seemed easier to keep things close to my chest. That didn't help my recovery at all, and I've found that although being honest can be horrible at the time, it feels like a weight has been lifted off once you start to talk about your worries. Reading 'quit-lit' kept me sane in the early days, reading and learning that I wasn't alone, that other people had been through and survived the same experiences as me. So during my battle with addiction I started and stopped writing every now and again, wanting to share, but terrified that I would be judged, or looked down upon. I was afraid by letting people in, that they would think I was crazy, and honestly, I still wondered if I really was crazy, I mean, what sort of women lets herself rely so much on the contents of a bottle? Those thoughts for once didn't stop me, and as I've always wanted to share my thoughts with other people I began to do it. It seems bizarre to me now, that I tell the readers of my blog many of my innermost thoughts. It's out there for all to see, and I feel so much better for it. Sharing, talking and understanding have really helped me work through my problems.

Who am I to write this though, you might ask? Well I'm a mum of four, a wife, 'a normal person', who from the outside certainly didn't look like an alcoholic. I've struggled with my mental health for years. Self-esteem and anxiety have always been a problem for me. When I look back and try to unpick it, I think the low self-esteem came first. I remember things from my childhood where I never felt quite good enough, but that continued once I was an adult. I've always felt a little misunderstood, but I know I often don't do a great job of trying to explain myself either. I've come to realise I'm better writing my thoughts down, my fingers seem to be more coherent than my voice does!

Drinking seemed normal for me, as it does for many people. Everyone I knew drank and mostly they seemed to do it to excess. It was very much the thing they used to relax, but mostly to have fun with. It seemed that there were very little situations where those I knew had fun without alcohol, and in some ways I actually looked down on the people who chose not to drink. I couldn't see how they could have a good time without alcohol, so I decided they were missing out. It's taken me a very long time to realise that isn't the case.

Once I had finally accepted my problem and admitted it to myself, I was ashamed about it, but I'll go into that more later on. I didn't want to talk to anyone about it, because I was afraid that they either wouldn't get it, or they'd think I was being dramatic. Those I did try to talk to seemed to brush it off, but I did have a few people comment that it was disappointing that I wouldn't be able to drink anymore. I don't think they really believed I was an alcoholic, and more than once I was encouraged to just get my drinking under control. If they'd been in my position they might have known that ship sailed a long time ago. I've been told that it was a shame I couldn't enjoy a 'nice drink' anymore; but I do enjoy nice drinks, they just don't have alcohol in them nowadays. In the end, it was easier to keep things to myself, if I really had to tell people I would, but I didn't go too much into the ins and outs of it, because I felt ashamed and embarrassed to be honest. It was hard, and harder still to say things that weren't going to be understood. It challenged my resolve and made me question myself. Now I'm stronger I remind myself that it isn't anyone's fault if they don't understand, that it isn't their problem and to be honest, they don't have to understand. No one else does, this is about me, not them. But it would be easier for me if everyone did.

One day, three years into sobriety I sat down and wrote a piece for my blog. I'd been playing again with a little bit of writing and publishing my posts on blog. My husband was supportive of me, but was worried how I would take criticism from others, so I was careful with what I wrote. I'm good enough at criticising myself without hearing other people's well-intentioned constructive criticism. Most of my posts were about day to day events, like my running or a yoga class. All important, but not hugely life changing. I hadn't realised they were warming me up for what came next. For the first time when I sat down, I wrote about the real thoughts and feelings I had about my addiction, the denial, the doubt, the feeling of fear about giving up my favourite drink, it all came out, and I posted it on my Facebook page. I didn't expect a lot. My page only had about ten followers and it felt safe to do it. I didn't have my surname on it, or invite any people I knew to like it as I preferred the anonymity at the time, it allowed me the freedom to say largely what I wanted to without worrying too much, although back then I was still somewhat careful as I wasn't sure what the reaction I'd get would be.

At the time I was heavily involved with my running club, The Lonely Goats. Random as it might sound, it is a national running club which at the time had about ten thousand members, it's gone up considerably since, as there was an article in Runners World magazine that encouraged a lot of new members. Although based predominantly online, it is a real club designed for those who don't get to club meetings or don't want to run with others.

As you might have guessed, me running with a big group wasn't an option, so I favoured the online option. We chat online about anything and everything and everyone is so supportive, it's a safe place. I'd never posted openly about my addiction, but I was beginning to reply to comments and posts left by other people and trying to be supportive to them. This one night, feeling brave, having just shared my post on my page I also shared it with them. I just wanted to know what they thought. Here's what I wrote…

Bear with me, this is a long one…

About six years ago, I wondered if I had a drink problem. I knew I drank a lot, but my husband also enjoyed a beer in the evening and it seemed normal to have one or two drinks in the evening to relax after a long day at work and stress with the kids. The thing was, I had a good job and a tidy house, I had happy kids and things were okay, so I decided I was being silly, and that I was fine. It's easy for me to worry about silly things due to my anxiety so I put it down to that.

About five years ago, I wondered again. By this time I'd got a different job. I'd told myself if I had further to drive, I'd have to get up earlier, therefore I'd drink less. I made a great friend at work, she'd talk with me in the mornings, maybe one of us or both of us would feel a little worse for wear. We'd encourage each other to have a night without, and we'd both mean it, but we worked in stressful roles, and each day was fraught. (Not an excuse!) By the evening, we'd be on the phone to each other reassuring each other that it was just one glass. It never was.

I read a book, it was dedicated to the women for whom one glass was never enough and always too many. That was me. One glass became two or three, and before long, two bottles of white wine every night. Every night. Fourteen bottles minimum in the recycling, just for me. But my house was clean, I had a job and a husband, happy kids. I couldn't have a problem. I just 'liked' a drink. Even when I was on my own.

About four years ago I hit rock bottom. I've always had difficulties with anxiety, and depression. I've never felt like I fitted in that well with anyone, except that is my husband, my rock who has stood by me through everything, and believe me, I haven't made things easy for him. I spoke to him, more than once over the years about drinking, and the amount I drank. He supported me, and together we'd abstain for a few days, managing about three by memory. I found this super challenging but I'd do it just about and then having proved that I could do without, I'd have a drink to celebrate. We live in a culture where alcohol is everywhere, you drink to celebrate, to relax, to commiserate, because you've had a hard day, because you've had an easy day. The list is endless, and it makes stopping hard, because everyone else is doing it. I never drank in the day, I hate to admit I was possibly still a little drunk in the morning from the amount I'd had the night before, but I never drank before 6pm. Then it became 5pm, then 4pm. It's a slippery slope. I hated wine at this point. I hated the hold it had over me, I couldn't reconcile how much I hated something I wanted so badly. Nothing was the same without it, I couldn't relax, I couldn't be calm. It was my saviour, to know I'd made it through the day and I could have my reward. It was strange though when the reward never seemed enough and then when I started to forget. My family would remind me of things I had said or done, but I had no recollection. I felt like I was losing my mind, my only constant was my bottle or two of wine. I stopped going out. It was work, home, kids, wine. I knew something needed to change.

I shut myself away one day and phoned a support group for help. I was at the end of the line and needed help. I couldn't do it on my own anymore. I played out the worst case scenarios of what would happen now I'd admitted I needed help. It terrified me. What I wasn't expected was a three month wait for help, and when it came, being told in a meeting to keep drinking. As I was drinking so much at the time, it would have been dangerous to stop. This only confused me further, I was so angry then, at myself, at wine, at life, but mostly myself for letting the situation get so bad.

Eventually I had cut down enough to be prescribed Antabuse from the doctor. Effectively if you take it and then drink you'll be really very sick. Taking that gave me back a little of the control. I knew that if I willingly took that, I'd not be able, (without risking my life), to drink. It was the first time, in a long time, that I felt a little bit in control.

Recovery was the hardest thing in the world I have ever done. It was also the best thing. I've been sober for over three years now and I know that I am 100% me all the time, any mistakes I make, any stupid things I say, that's me, not wine saying them. I've not only had to stop drinking, but basically relearn the way I approach things. Alcohol is so ingrained into our society that we assume there is something wrong with someone when they don't drink, unless they are the designated driver. It took me a long time to see that I wasn't boring because I wasn't drinking. It was also hard to find something to do with all the time I had now. Sitting mindlessly in front of the TV in the evening was not enough anymore. Harder still was dealing with anxiety on a daily basis, rather than drinking to keep my mind sedated. Nowadays that is the tricky thing, alcohol played such a part in being a buffer for me, I didn't have to over think things because I couldn't, self-medicating calmed me. Now there is no buffer, it's just me, doing the best I can, and living with the consequences. I try my best, but like everyone, I do make mistakes. Day by day, I am getting there. It is certainly easier now, even though I'm still caught off guard by old thought patterns.

To anyone out there who is going through something similar, keep going, it is worth it, even though it is hard. Remember too, be kind to yourself.

Thanks for reading!
xx

I was expecting maybe one or two comments, I thought I'd have criticism mixed in with any positivity. What I received instead was a huge out pouring of love for me and my post. I was amazed so many people understood. So many people could relate, and I touched more people than I could imagine. I made sure I answered every single comment, it really mattered to me to connect with like-minded people; it still does. The likes on my page grew and I continued to reply. Then at some point in the evening I made my mistake, and posted a reply from my private account instead of from my page. I'm not sure how, I think in my excitement I just rushed, but when I did that, it must have given a notification to my friends list. Suddenly instead of the safety of my running club, people I knew in the real world were commenting too. Until then I'd pretty much isolated myself from friends and acquaintances. I didn't tell anyone besides my close family about my battle. I didn't think anyone else would understand, and I didn't want to look like I was after attention. I didn't know who I could trust, so I didn't trust anyone. Instead, I cut myself off. I didn't see my old friends and I had deleted anyone from my social media friends lists who I felt didn't know the 'real' me, the one who had been hidden for so long. My rule was, if I wouldn't say hello in the street, they were removed from my friends list. It was a safety net for me really, but suddenly, and without warning, I let everyone in, and told the world everything. My post was shared and liked and commented on by so many people, and everyone was so kind. It was amazing. Scary, but amazing! Some of my family even read it, which was quite embarrassing for me, but I think it helped, after that, they seemed to understand at least a little more than they had before.

So after that, I tried to make sure all my posts were relevant to my growing audience. I began to tell them about everything, because much as it defined who I was now, my addiction wasn't the only part of me. I was also a wife, a mum, a runner, a yogi and I began to share it all. The more I wrote the more I worried that I would run out of things to write, but there was always something waiting to trigger a thought for me to write about. It was strange, I was so private in so many ways and yet here I was opening up to people I didn't even know and letting them in to my thoughts and feelings. I was almost three years sober but still unsure of myself, and yet, all at once, with the sharing I did online, I began to feel better. Writing helped me work through things, it helped me process and understand myself and hearing from others made me feel like I was making a difference. I found it so much easier to write than to explain how I felt and it was lovely to hear from other people, not only those who found my writing helpful, but those that wanted advice, or those encouraging me. They say that writing is cathartic, but I had never experienced anything like this.

I felt like I was getting to know myself again, and letting others hear my voice again.

CHAPTER 2
THE BEGINNING

I think all things should start at the beginning. It's hard to pinpoint where the beginning is for someone who has always 'enjoyed' a drink, at least since I was a teenager. I don't remember when exactly I had my first drink, but I do remember having one well before the legal age, especially when we had people around to our house. It was just what the adults did and I wanted to fit in. I felt grown up and sophisticated even if I didn't like it. Honestly, I didn't enjoy it, but I persevered far more than I would or did with other things like coffee. I wanted to like coffee too, it seemed like a far more grown up drink than the tea that I'd always enjoyed. But, I didn't like it and so apart from the odd cup here or there when I wanted to look cool, I didn't drink it. It wasn't the same for alcohol. I persevered and I kept trying, because it mattered to me to fit in and look grown up. There were a few times that I snuck a bottle of orange topped with up with vodka into school to 'help' me through a drama class. I think in hindsight, it was probably more to get noticed and fit in. I started clubbing when I was about fifteen. My friends and I never had trouble getting into night clubs or getting served with alcohol, so that's what we did every Friday and Saturday night. Sometimes we went to special themed nights out in the week too, I remember many 70's nights at a local club that isn't there any more, that seemed fun at the time, but wouldn't be my scene now. When I think back I wonder how I could afford it, but then I remember that I rarely had to pay for drinks. There was always someone who was happy to buy them for us, or special offers so they cost next to nothing. Many a night I stayed with friends in town and got a lift home in the morning, it was just what we did, and at the time I thought it was fun. Even back then, right back at the beginning I drank too much. I didn't drink every night, but my friends and I all enjoyed a drink. We did it a lot, and it made us feel cool, like adults, even though we were only teenagers. There were plenty of nights where I took it too far, hangovers were fairly common at the weekends, but I was young and it was fun, even if wasn't legally allowed to drink yet. One night we had a party at a friends house on the beach as her family were out of town. I lost something in the sand and while looking for it, stumbled and fell down the sand dune rolling over a stone wall and into the river. It was funny, except I cut my legs quite badly. My friends couldn't find me and I had to climb back in through the kitchen window. I would be mortified doing something like that now, but then it just seemed funny. The night after I was going out with my friends, it was an early birthday celebration as I was going to be seventeen in the week. My girlfriends and I took a long time getting ready, trying to decide if I should wear long boots to cover my scrapes from the night before, but I decided to wear strappy shoes as normal. If things had been different and I spent my weekends in a different way then I wouldn't have met Lee. We lived fifty miles apart, he didn't come to Newquay often, mainly choosing the clubs in Plymouth at the time, but if he did it would be on a Friday. We were both out that Saturday with our separate groups of friends and by pure fluke we caught each others attention. It was obviously meant to be. We spent more time chatting than anything else and realised we had so much in common. I ditched my friends, and accepted his offer of a lift home. I didn't even think about how I was going to explain how I was home to my parents, but I got so much stick from my friends for not telling them where I was. They were worried because they hadn't met him yet and were unsure about whether he was a gentleman or not. They didn't need to worry, I was lucky and he very much is. We talked more over the phone throughout the week, and went out again the next weekend, each bringing a friend to break the ice as we had no friends in common.

Things moved pretty fast for Lee and I, we just clicked, and we talked all the time. I remember him being surprised even then that I sometimes drank alone. It just felt normal and a way to relax. Back then it was more often than not 'alcopops', just something to take the edge off before I went out or while I chatted to friends, and they all did the same. There were nights then when I drank too much and ended up being sick, but I didn't stop. One night I lost the group we were with and Lee found me outside the nightclub sitting on a shop window ledge. I never meant to end up the way I did, it was only ever supposed to be fun. I just didn't have a regulator when it came to drinking. One night we ended up getting into a fight in a night club. It wasn't something that had ever happened to me before, I wasn't that sort of person and neither was Lee, but it was drink fuelled and he tried to protect me. It was over a sofa I think, someone thought it was their seat and I didn't agree. I got pulled across the dance floor by my hair. It really hurt and we left the club straight after swearing we wouldn't go back. I remember bottles being thrown at us as we ran down the street. It was horrible, and the only time I have ever been in a situation like that.

Three months after we met, Lee and I settled down together. We got married and bought our house when I was eighteen and had our first baby, Joseph when I was nineteen. We didn't have much money, we'd had no time to save, despite how hard Lee worked, but I gave up work as it would have cost more for me to travel and put Joe into childcare than I got paid, so we tried to tighten up the purse strings. Although things were tight, we didn't want to drag out our expanding our family, and wanted the kids to be close together in age. We couldn't imagine having an older one and then starting again with a baby. On Joe's second birthday Katie was born, and the month before she was two, Barney joined us. It was hectic having three kids so young, so close in age and so busy, but I loved it. They were a handful, but one I was so proud to have. When Barn was two I went back to work, trying to find something that could fit around the children but something that made me feel I was contributing to the house too. It wasn't that being a Mum wasn't enough, because it was; it was just sometimes I felt like I had lost myself a little bit along the way and I wanted to feel like I was earning too. When you're a Mum it comes first, but without work, I wasn't sure who I was. Perhaps as I was so young I'd never really finished forming my identity. I'd made some friends at baby group when Joe was young, but I struggled to fit in. I didn't have much in common with the other mums that were my age. Many didn't have partners and were still out partying or in drinking, and back then I didn't want to, except on the odd occasion at home with Lee. I'm not judging, but we lived very different lives and I just wanted friends that had similar interests. On the other hand, the older mums, the ones I felt I had something in common with, looked down a little on me. They didn't see the relationship Lee and I had, and just saw the fact I was a teenage mum. It was a difficult time, because I just wanted to fit with similar people as the kids were growing up. I really just wanted friends.

My drinking gradually crept up over the years from something I did in a controlled and fun way to something that I relied on. I don't remember a time when something changed exactly, but I do remember a lovely holiday in 2007 where we drove down to Lake Annecy in France and we didn't drink at all for over a week. It wasn't hard not to either, it was just something we didn't think about doing. We swam in the lake with the children, it was hot, and yet when we climbed a nearby mountain they could play in the snow. As the time went on, I would never have been able to go that long without a drink. So it was definitely after that. In fact, the year after, in 2008, we went back, and took Lee's Mum and Dad with us to show them the place we had enjoyed so much. It was still a lovely holiday, but I spent a lot more time drinking and it wasn't just because I was on holiday with my in-laws! Every day involved a supermarket trip to buy food but always involved wine too.

I'm going to go back to 2009, for me the year that things started to change, when things got worse and the 'one too many' became very often. It's when I began to rely on something which had used to just be fun so I guess this is a good place to start.

CHAPTER 3
2009

When I first began to wonder if I had a drinking problem I doubted myself. People like me didn't have drinking problems. I had a husband, 3 kids who were loved, clean and looked after, a job and a house with a mortgage. Putting it down to overthinking I carried on the way I was for a long time. Too long. Like I said, I overthink, I always have, so thinking my anxiety was at work, and of course that if I talked to anyone about it that they would probably think I was over-reacting or attention seeking, it was easier to keep my concerns to myself and just carry on. As I've said before, alcohol seemed to surround me and seemed the thing to rely on for so many reasons, the coping strategy for stress, the reward for everything else. I agree that it is a way for someone to enjoy themselves, but it seemed to be the only thing, and a way to excuse it. I think the reassurance that everyone around me all did it, made it okay, and so I grew up thinking that it was what adults did.

After I was married I never used to drink at home, especially on my own, but gradually it crept up on me. Lee worked hard, he always had done. He was the only breadwinner for us for a long time, and we liked to do things to the house and live as well as we could. He had worked his way up from the bottom of the ladder to become a director in his company. When that happened it was a changing point really, his long hours became longer as he was able to drive the company forward, and of course wanted to make it the best it could be. As well as working long hours, he worked away often and it was hard, as it meant I was often at home with the kids on my own. I'm not excusing my drinking, or blaming him, I know there are many families out there in a similar position, but it was hard at times. We made sacrifices as other people do, hoping one day it would pay off and we would one day be in a better financial situation than we were currently. The problem, (not that I would ever change it) with being married young, was that we didn't have a huge amount of savings behind us. We were lucky to be able to buy our own home shortly after we got married, and before Joe was born in 2001. The house was run down and we spent a lot of time on it, never paying for trades, but doing all the work ourselves, it grew with the family, but money always seemed to go quicker than it came in, and so extra hours were always needed to help us get through, or pay for the extra bits and pieces we wanted.

Life got busier, three kids with less than four years between them, a dog, a full time job, a husband who was extremely busy with work and a house to look after. More and more often I began to pour myself 'just the one' before Lee came home in the evening. Sometimes, he would phone to tell me he would be late and tell me to have a glass of wine to relax. It was just what everyone seemed to do. It had often been a tiring day or a hard day, there was always a reason, and I justified it to myself because it seemed everyone else did it too. Every advert told me so, and in my favourite TV programme of the time 'Desperate Housewives', most of the women also used drinking as a way to relax. Okay, one of them was an alcoholic, but that was unusual I told myself. It seemed okay to drink. It seemed normal. More than that, it made me feel exciting, grown up, like I was fitting in. Looking back, I'm not really sure who it was that I wanted to fit in with.

Occasionally we would talk with friends and I remember being surprised to hear that they didn't drink every night. It was such a normality to me, I couldn't imagine drinking anything else. A cup of tea in the evening seemed boring, an old persons thing to do. I know that isn't right, and now there is nothing I like more than a cup of tea, but back then wine was so ingrained in my life I didn't know how to do without it. Anything other than wine seemed wrong. Buying multiple bottles of wine almost every day became just as normal as buying milk or toilet rolls, it was just a necessity. The only reason I could think for them not to drink like I did, was because they couldn't afford it. It didn't occur to me that they might choose not to. I couldn't imagine why anyone would choose that.

Over time though, the more I thought about drinking, the more it worried me and the more I realised I had come to rely on it. I began to subconsciously plan things to do to try to counteract my drinking without making it obvious. I wasn't going to admit to anyone that I liked drinking too much, back then I couldn't even admit it to myself, it was just a niggling thought in the back of my mind. The idea of stopping was beginning to dawn on me but I couldn't imagine what life without wine would look like. It was easier to try not to confront it and instead put things in the way to try to help me out. For a long time I had wanted to teach, I hadn't gone to university after college, but I'd always been interested in going back and when the opportunity came up to do a degree with Open University alongside everything else, it seemed a great idea. It was a lot of money and a lot of work, but I was dedicated, and I hoped with needing to work in the evenings and weekends, that I would drink a little less. Not that I told anyone else that was part of my plan. I wanted to progress my career and I wanted to prove that I was clever, that I could do something besides being a mum and housewife. I knew I was good at those, and it mattered to me, but I wanted to prove myself to myself if that makes sense? So I scheduled it in alongside my job and the kids, and everything else.

At this time, I worked at a school so close I could walk there, two of our children also went there with the littlest going to the school next door. It meant I didn't worry about having too many drinks at night, because I didn't have to drive. I remember my Mum and Dad being doubtful that I could complete a degree, suggesting it might be too much for me along with everything else. I'm sure they didn't mean it negatively but that was how I took it. It felt like they expected me to fail before I'd even begun. At the same time, my mother-in-law told me that she thought I'd have to let some things go if I was going to take that on too. The problem is that especially back then, I took any comment like that as criticism and in my head, rather than think that they were all trying to help me, I took it as a challenge and went out to prove them all wrong.

I have a little bit of an obsessive nature, you see. It's not always a bad thing, but it does mean I struggle to let silly things slide by. In many ways, I think my nature is partly to blame for my dependency on alcohol. If I'd been a little bit more balanced and addressed my mental health sooner, I don't think I would have begun to self medicate in the first place.

Often, I know my habits are a bit daft, or at least would seem so to other people, but if I don't do them, I can't relax. It makes me feel physically uncomfortable. For example, the hoovering. I have to do it every day at least once without fail, normally before I go to work so the house is tidy when I get home, but then I often do it again when I get home. It doesn't matter if the house doesn't really need it, I just have to do it, even if the house has been empty in the time I've been at work. Some days it can be a lot, the other day it was about five times, other times I can leave it at the one. I know the first time can be justified, as I like to keep the house neat and tidy, but then if I see anything on the floor I have to do it again. I can't even just do the bit that is 'dirty', I have to do the whole house again. It's frustrating, and the only one that makes me do it is myself. I can justify it normally as I want to keep the house tidy in case anyone stops by, but that isn't always the case, and in the evenings especially, I wish I could just leave it and relax.

So I often took things personally and misconstrued comments that were supposed to be supportive as criticism. Instead of seeing them in the way they were intended, instead it just fired me up to take on more and not let things slide. I felt like I wanted to prove everyone wrong, and show them I could do it. I put more and more pressure on and expected more from myself each day. Of course at the end of a long day, that relief was always waiting for me as I poured a glass or two of wine. No one else even remembered the comments they'd made, they certainly wouldn't now, I am sure, but I still felt that I had something to prove.

Somewhere in this time I visited the doctor for advice about my mental health. It wasn't the first time, I'd been before and had been given anti-depressants. I hadn't agreed with the diagnosis, for me I felt that my issues were much more ingrained and had been there since at least my teen years, although the change in circumstances around the time of having a baby possibly did bring things to a head. Before that, I had heard comments once or twice that I was a sad child, but I'm not sure. It seemed the GP just wanted to give me a quick fix. I came away with my anti-depressants but couldn't face taking them, it didn't seem justified, I didn't think I was bad enough and once again, I worried that it might be thought I was attention-seeking, so I stopped after a few days. It seemed like such a big thing, I couldn't imagine that I really needed them, I was okay most of the time, I just had a wobble every now and again that I found really difficult. The stigma around taking anti-depressants back then felt very different to what it is now. I felt like a failure, I felt palmed off by the doctor and I felt misunderstood again. I'm not sure back then if I expressed how muddled I felt, I certainly didn't when I was younger, I just thought everyone felt the same way I did.

Some months or a year later I went back and tried again. This time I was told the only option was to see a therapist. They told me very matter-of-factly that they had given me anti-depressants before and they hadn't worked so there would be no point in trying again. I tried to explain, and tell them I didn't take them, but no one seemed to listen and so I came away with a referral to a therapist. That didn't go so well either. I saw a lady who was perfectly nice, she just didn't seem to understand. It seems there are a lot of people out there who don't quite get mental health problems like anxiety, they suggest you can just stop worrying or overthinking, they say you can stop something you don't even understand yourself. I really hope that things are better now, they must be as things are definitely a lot more spoken about now than they were back then. So, I saw this lady, who listened, gave me a book about obsessive compulsive disorder, and told me I should stop hoovering the house so much. I did try to tell her that to me, trying to avoid things like the hoovering or excessively wiping the worktop were actually physically uncomfortable, it was like not being allowed to go to the toilet when you need to. She didn't get it, instead she laughed as if I was joking and said that I needed to stop. She even asked me why I needed to do it. But it's hard to explain something when you don't understand it yourself. It was painful, and didn't help. If I had been able to stop, I would have done. I just couldn't. She asked me why it was so important, and why I felt I needed to do it, but I couldn't answer because I didn't know. It was just something that made me feel settled, I had certain things that I felt needed to be done, and until they were, I couldn't relax. I knew I drove Lee mad on Sunday afternoons. All he would want to do was sit and relax for a bit after a long week at work but as much as I wanted to, I would be running around tidying and cleaning. I knew it wasn't imperative but would feel uncomfortable until I'd done everything, sometimes repeating things I had already done. If I didn't achieve what I felt was expected of me, I worried I would be seen as lazy but once the jobs were done to my satisfaction it was like a switch had been flicked off in my brain and things settled.

I wanted to get a handle on my worrying and my compulsive behaviour, I'd asked for help, but got nowhere. It made it so much worse for me, it was like no one really believed me, or that the way I felt wasn't bad enough for help, and yet the feelings I had didn't go away. In the end, I turned to the only thing that had been able to help me, pouring myself more wine. Sundays became more relaxing, we'd put on a family film, have a mid-afternoon dinner and crash out with the kids in the lounge. It was great fun to be together and relaxing, and of course it meant that I could have a drink a lot earlier in the day. So I didn't go back to the doctors. I decided I would manage by myself, I'd asked for help and they couldn't help me. I didn't need them.

CHAPTER 4
2010

That slippery slope was always there for me. I often thought I'd have 'a' glass of wine, but one never quite hit the mark so I'd have another one. By the time I'd had a couple any resolve I made would go out the window and I'd forget I was worried about limits. There was always the next day when I could start to worry again. There was quite a lot of talk at the time of binge drinking which sounded like a worry, before then I don't remember hearing of such a thing. I remember it being explained that it was when people went out and got hammered at the weekend, drinking to oblivion. At the time this felt like a great justification to me for my drinking, I actually convinced myself that it was better that I drank regularly as it meant my body was more used to it. Looking back, I know this is ridiculous, but at the time it made me feel better, like I didn't have a worry, and therefore I could carry on doing as I was doing, without any problem. To be honest, back then I didn't think I was making excuses. I didn't see that I had a problem, I just thought I liked a drink, and lots of people I knew seemed to as well. I hadn't realised that I created excuses to validate my drinking and make it seem okay in my own mind. Over time, that only got worse.

Time went by and I decided I wanted a new job. Working where I had been was great for many reasons, I could walk to work, I could drop the kids at school, I could pop home in my lunch hour to let the dog out. It worked, and yet it didn't. I felt I was too close to the kids, it didn't feel fair on them and to be honest the lack of space between us stressed me out a lot. Every time my eldest was in trouble, and it was often as he was a nine year old boy, doing silly things that boys do, all the staff and children were keen to tell me what he had done. The main problem seemed to be 'rolling down the banks' - I am not kidding, rolling down the grassy banks in the field was a punishable offence. If he was caught, he would be made to stand against the wall in the school hall for the rest of the lunchtime, missing out on sunny days playing because it was against the rules. I even spoke to the headteacher about it, but was reassured that while I might not complain about a dirty uniform, other parents would, and so the rule and the punishment stayed. Of course, when he was seen there, I had a stream of people ready to tell me that he was in trouble, rather than just leave us both alone. I was already harder on my kids than other children, to make sure no-one thought I was favouring them, but that in itself wasn't fair on my kids. I wanted a job where we could go home and tell each other the things we had done without already knowing. They missed out and I didn't like it. I wanted a job that was similar, but different; the problem was, I didn't want to work in just another school, and if I was doing the same job, it would most likely pay the same which wouldn't allow for me having to travel. My job was working with children whose behaviour could challenge the traditional confines of a classroom. Some of the children had already been excluded previous times from education, some were aggressive, some just didn't like being in a classroom. I was patient and didn't scare easy, I was good at working with them, I just didn't want to do it around my own kids anymore.

One day I saw a job advertised for exactly what I did already, except instead of in a school, it was working in a unit specifically with children who could no longer be in mainstream education. The role was to support these kids and get them back into schools. On the spur of the moment I applied, it was just a little drive, but I thought this would help with my mission to drink less without admitting to anyone else that I was beginning to realise I had a problem.

I applied well before the deadline and knew on paper at least that I was more than qualified for the job, but in reality, I knew that often employers looking for candidates to fit roles specifically like these already had their preferred option lined up. I didn't hear anything for a while, actually it was a couple of months, and I had almost forgotten about it when I had a call asking me to come in for an interview. I'd pretty much talked myself out of it, I think when I don't think something is going to work out, I almost put myself off as a way of protecting myself. I didn't pick up the call as I was actually out on a school trip, but when I got back and listened to the voicemail, I had a bit of time to think about it and even spoke to my boss about it. Under the advice of my headteacher at the time I went to look around the unit, and decided it wasn't really for me, the staff weren't that welcoming, and it didn't seem like the sort of place I wanted to work. Having made that decision, I went to the interview anyway, using it for practice if nothing else. It was bizarre, walking in, and not caring how it went - it was actually quite liberating, and they definitely got the authentic me, rather than one trying to impress! During the actual meeting, while I was being interviewed by three big bosses and a lead teacher who I'll call Alison, I found out that the whole staffing structure was changing, and all of the staff I had met were being replaced. At this point though, I was past caring about it, and left the interview to meet Lee at the pub in his lunch hour. That was something we used to enjoy doing, he often worked through his lunch hours, except for a Friday, a day I didn't work, when I'd go and meet him in the pub across the road from his office. It was our thing, and another excuse to have a little drink here and there.

Lee and I were sitting in the pub, not long after my interview when my phone rang, and of course as I hadn't been too worried about it, I was offered the job, much to my surprise. I didn't know what to do then, and told them, much to their disappointment, that I'd think about it. I didn't know what else to say, but I was told afterwards that my response hadn't gone down well. I wasn't sure what to do, I'd had second thoughts about the travelling amongst other things and so I went to speak to my headteacher. He told me that there was obviously a reason I had gone for it and expressed in no uncertain terms that I should accept it, and so I did.

Everything changed with this new job. I worked closely in a unit with two other women, Alison and another lady I'll call Mel. Working with a small group of children our aim was to nurture and get them ready to go back into school. We were working on filling the gaps in social and emotional development of children that may have difficult backgrounds. I was dropped in at the deep end, supporting children and their families and advising school staff. It was stressful. Some schools didn't want to know and only wanted me in to effectively babysit the child while we were on their premises. I'd be stuck watching and trying to engage with quite aggressive children with no support but a whole host of people ready to blame me if something went wrong. Hard wouldn't begin to cover what it was like. Every day felt like a battle, we had troubled kids, troubled families and unsupportive schools. There were a couple of exceptions to that rule, but they were few and far between. We had violence, we had kids run, we had to call the police for our own protection or that of the other kids and for the same reason we had to exclude children. We were trained to safely restrain the children when necessary to protect not only the child themselves but also that of others in the building and at one point it seemed every day involved us having to use these techniques. The children we had were in crisis and when their behaviour escalated it was like dominoes, one would trigger the other and we were on a constant state of high alert.

It was a hard job, but at the same time it had it's perks. Mel and Alison became two of my closest friends. It was strange working in such close proximity for much of the day we joked that we began to think alike, and while Alison didn't drink much if at all, Mel was on a similar level to me. We often had 'team building' lunches at the pub, just the three of us, and a couple of glasses, obviously not when we had to go back to the children, only on the days we had planning scheduled or the afternoon off. It was a bonus.

Mel like me had a lot of responsibilities on her, and no one else to share them with, but that is her story to tell, and not mine. Needless to say her day often ended in a glass or two bottles of wine just like mine did. Some days I would try to broach it with her, I felt if I said I was worried and someone agreed, they would tell me and I would have to do something about it, but instead, she reassured me that I was fine, that she was too. So we carried on. We weren't a great influence on each other, we definitely made it easier for each other to drink, or at least, she did me, to be honest, I don't know what situation she was in with drink really, I felt sometimes, that she would be dramatic about it but could leave it alone far more easily than I could. No one really knows quite what is going on in someone else's mind though do they? Certainly although I spoke to her, I don't think she really understood how worried about myself I was really. Not until the end anyway. It was one of those things, although I tested the water, I couldn't admit to myself what a mess I was in, and if I couldn't do that, how was I supposed to admit it to anyone else?

Things began to get harder. The job was stressful, I drank more wine. My husband was at work, I drank more wine. The kids are in bed, so I drank more wine. What had once been a reward just became a normality. Most people would go home and put the kettle on. I went home and got the corkscrew out.

I talked to Mel more and more. Coming to work with a headache and taking painkillers to start the day was becoming more frequent, as did drinking a can of Coke on my way in instead of having breakfast. We would make a pact in the morning, that that evening we would both not drink, that we would have one or two nights off a week and support and encourage each other to get through it. She would tell me that not drinking made her so grumpy she would put her kids to bed and then go to bed herself. Often at 7pm. Wine ruled us. But we had each other and our pact, - it should have helped, to have someone else who at least understood a little bit. Alison was always surprised that we drank most (every) night as she didn't, mind you she didn't drink tea or coffee either, so we just decided she was a bit strange. Why wouldn't you drink a glass of wine in the evening? Everyone did it, it was fine and doing the job we did, with everything else going on meant that we deserved it. Of course though, Mel and I were cutting down. We were so supportive of each other that each evening we would phone one another and check the other was okay. This was normally about 4:30pm so not long after I had arrived at home. We would remind ourselves of our pact, and then reassure each other that just for tonight, one drink would be okay, that it was just one. But that one was never enough and suddenly it was two, or three, or more. Mostly more. Often while we were still on the phone. So the next day we would start again, the reassurance that we were okay, the reasoning that we deserved it, the support that we were both okay. However much I loved Mel as a friend, I question now, how much worse this made me, how much this facilitated my problem and helped it become more ingrained in my life. I'm not blaming my friend or my lifestyle, or my job, I just know that these factors all contributed to the way I was and what I became.

Things carried on in the same way for the four years I worked there. The kids I worked with got more extreme, and the schools and families were challenging. Combining this with my busy home life, wine became more and more a part of my life. It was nice to tick things off the list, I always made sure things were done before I drank, but then when I sat down in the evening, I felt like I could finally relax. All day long, it didn't matter how stressful, how challenging, how upsetting, as long as I could get through it, it would result in several glasses to relax. So that's how things were. Lee worked more and more, often project managing installations all over the country, and when he was at home he still worked long hours. He was so keen to do everything he could to help the company to progress and be successful and I didn't mind, I really wanted to be supportive, it was just hard picking up everything else at home, and of course, evening after evening did result in wine. I saw it as my reward. I didn't realise how much I relied on it to quieten my mind. I mean I suppose I did, on some level I must have, otherwise, why would I continue to buy and pour it? But I felt, as long as everything was done, the house was tidy, the kids were safe in bed and we could afford it, why not?

CHAPTER 5
2011

Adverts and TV programmes only seem to reinforce the message that alcohol is a reward, so that is the way I still perceived it. A welcome relief to a hard day, you know the sort of thing, where you get home from work and chill out with that nice cold glass of wine. Often the people in the adverts looked picture perfect too, with wonderful hair, but recreating that part of the advert wasn't quite so important to me. All that was important was the glass of wine. The problem for me is that one glass was never enough. I had a conversation with one of my younger sons last year and he told me that he never intended to have a 'problem' with drinking or drugs or anything like that, he and his friends just wanted to enjoy but not get carried away. I laughed. His innocence surprised me and I told him so. Once I'd stopped laughing, I even asked him, "Who on earth would choose to have a drinking problem?" I certainly didn't go looking for one. It wasn't like something I decided so went shopping to fulfil my need. It crept up slowly and infiltrated every area of my life before I even knew it was there. There was no choosing and no real awareness. Once I was a 'normal' drinker, and then I wasn't.

My husband describes my drinking as not having a cap. I think it's quite a good way of describing it. I loved the idea of having a drink, whether it was in the evening at home or on a night out. It's just I couldn't stop once I got started. One glass was never enough. Well, it might have been in the early years, before I worked my tolerance up, but I don't ever remember stopping at one. It took a few glasses to even begin to feel something. So I had to drink more, although I will admit, that once I had poured that first glass, and could see it on the side in the kitchen, I relaxed, just a little, it was good to know it was there. I was twitchy until then you see, wanting something, needing something, and felt the relief as soon as I had opened the bottle to fill that glass. I even used to plan it as I was driving on my way home.

The problem with having no cap is that it ruins things. You don't realise, or at least, I didn't realise how drunk I was until it was too late. I never seemed to just get tipsy anymore and there were times I prided myself on being able to carry on regardless. At a house party one year, I was sloshed super early, I steadily drank as people bustled about me and when I finally moved the room did too. It wasn't pleasant, but making myself sick often worked as a way to keep going. Not pretty but the truth, and soon I was back enjoying the party again. I actually felt good because I always stopped at alcohol. Others at the party began to do much harder substances, and I was proud I didn't. It didn't even occur to me to try, so I took it as more reassurance that I was okay and drinking as I did, felt like a badge of strength, being able to carry on, regardless.

I thought I hid my drinking so well. I didn't. It's embarrassing now to think of how many people probably knew of my problem, or at least knew I drank too much, before I did. I thought drinking made me the life and soul of the party, I was fun, I was uninhibited. I talked and chatted to people I couldn't have done before I had a drink, and yet, it wasn't really me was it? If it was I would have been able to do it without the drink. I came to rely on it to get by in social situations, only in the evening mind you, but of course, the more I drank, the more I needed to drink and the situation got worse. At a Christmas works party, years ago now, I thought I was entertaining, I thought I was doing a great job talking to the guests and making them feel welcome. In some ways I probably was, but it wasn't until I swayed a little too much and spilled a glass of red wine down my (thankfully black) dress, that I cottoned on to the fact that rather than being interested in my conversation, the man I was talking to was more interested in staring at my boobs. It was unfortunate that I had to be told that though. I felt like such an idiot afterwards. A naive idiot.

More often that I would like, perfectly good nights out (or in) were ruined by my inability to know when I had had too much to drink. I never knew it was coming until it was too late, and I would probably have told you that you were wrong if you tried to warn me. I always knew best, and I did like my wine. Most people learn from their experiences, but I struggled to do that. Often after a heavy night out, waking up with a sore head should have been reason enough to take a break for a day or two at least, but not me. I saw slowing down as a weakness, as a reason to admit I was drinking too much. I wouldn't ever admit I had a hangover, as I didn't want anyone to suggest it was because of my drinking, I just tried to push through, often drinking a can of Coke on the way to work to help me out. No matter what day it was I got up, brushed myself down and carried on where I had left off. It wasn't so much 'hair of the dog' as I didn't drink in the day, except for Sunday lunchtimes occasionally when we were out for lunch, but taking a break was not something that had a place in my life.

There were other occasions too, like the night out with friends where I had one too many and burst into tears in the middle of the restaurant, and had to leave. I perked up later and returned to the table, but when everyone else switched to softer drinks I carried on with the wine, still matching them glass for glass, until I was sick in an alleyway having run away from all the drama. I thought it was funny at the time. Of course afterwards I was embarrassed, but I could brush it off as a one off, even though it wasn't at all. A night in with other friends was supposed to be fun too, we walked to their house as they lived locally. Of course there were a few drinks, but we were having dinner with them, so we ordered a takeaway and sat down to chat while we waited for it to be delivered. I don't think it was a special night, but something had happened and the food took much longer than normal. I don't even remember getting drunk, but I know that suddenly I felt ill. I was hot, and feeling sick and had to go out and sit in the garden. It was a horrible feeling hearing the three of them laughing together and knowing I had ruined the night, I couldn't eat anything and we went home early, and yet, it still wasn't enough for me to stop drinking. These occurrences just became more and more frequent.

My leaving party when I left my previous school was another night I wish I could erase. It was the end of term, as well as the end of my time there, and the kids and staff finished early. We decided to skip lunch and walk to the local Wetherspoons for a late lunch and drinks. Of course, that was fatal for me, I tried to be clever and order something substantial because I knew that I would be drinking a fair bit, but I always failed to limit what I put away, compared to other people. I saw it as fair game, if they had two soft drinks, I could have two wines. Gradually people slipped away, the sensible ones at least, leaving fewer and fewer of us together, and we moved from one pub to another. I have a photo of two of the ladies I was with lying in the middle of the road, where they'd fallen after having a cuddle. I was proud it wasn't me, and that again reinforced that I was okay. One of the women had a bit of a friendly rivalry with me. She was nice enough, but liked people to know that she had more, or did more than other people, and when we were sat at a table I decided to call her out on it, I'd just had enough of listening to her being the authority on everything. I guess the wine I had been drinking removed my inhibitions. But it ended badly, with her storming off to the toilets, saying she was going to hit me and me thinking, "What the hell?" I decided to leave, it was more drama than I had wanted, and I couldn't be bothered with people threatening me. So I stood to leave, but another woman wouldn't let me have my bag. It was more than frustrating, I just wanted to go, and felt cornered, but I couldn't get my bag. She wanted me to stay to chat and thought the other woman was joking. In the end I left, leaving all my stuff there, and walked home alone on my own in the dark. Lee was shocked when I got there, disappointed in me and in my friends for the way the evening had ended, and I was upset, in floods of tears as I tried to explain what had happened. Shortly after, the three women turned up on my doorstep, and came to apologise, telling me they had meant nothing bad. I soon bounced back, and we had many more drinks at home, before two of my friends left, leaving just me and Lee with the woman I'd argued with. Later on her husband turned up to join us. I didn't really think about the fact that Lee had work the next morning, and we soon were pulling out Singstar on the PlayStation and having a great time. They didn't leave until the very early hours of the morning. That hangover lasted over two days. It was probably one of the worst ones I have ever had. I could barely function, and was in a proper state. Somehow I managed to convince myself that I was ill as well as having a hangover, but I was in no fit state for anything. It just added to my regrets.

CHAPTER 6
2012

For years my wisdom teeth had been threatening to come through, from memory they started when I was about eighteen, but never quite finished the job. I had a little corner of two of them, but no more as the rest were under my teeth with no space left for them. As the years went by I gradually began to get more and more headaches and eventually mentioned to the dentist that they were causing me problems. I knew in all likelihood that they would have to come out, but I put off finding out for sure. Like a baby teething, I enjoyed chewing things, especially a packet of Skittles. It felt so good at the time, but afterwards was agony! My dentist referred me to the hospital, because they were compacted, and he couldn't advise beyond the fact that they'd need to come out. I'd been lucky enough to have reasonably good teeth in that they were strong, and although crooked, I had never had to have fillings or anything. The worst experience I had was having to have four teeth out and a brace fitted when I was a teenager, so this was all new.

Having never had treatment before for anything serious, I tried to live with the headaches from my wisdom teeth for a long time, hoping they would somehow sort themselves out. I really didn't want to go into hospital for surgery of any kind. The only visits I had ever had before were to have our children, and so I felt strange about opting to go in and have a procedure that wasn't really health related, even if the dentist was recommending it and I told it would stop my increasingly frequent headaches and toothaches. I wasn't even going to know too much about it as they wanted to put me under general anaesthetic for the surgery. On an appointment prior to the procedure I saw a headline on a newspaper telling how someone had found they had cancer when they routinely had a tooth removed. Logically I knew not to believe everything I read in the papers and yet, it played on my mind. I worried that the doctors might find something wrong with me too, the more I tried to reassure myself, the more I worried, and frustratingly, I knew there was only one real reason for my worry. Wine.

In the end the surgery itself was fine, I went into hospital, had my wisdom teeth extracted and was discharged the same day. I do remember waking up to the surgeon laughing at me because it there was so little space in my mouth, they found the extraction difficult, but it was all in good humour. Lee drove me to the hospital and stayed with me before bringing me home again, but obviously had to go back to work the next day. I had been signed off work for two weeks which was fine, but as he was working away again, I had to drive the kids to school. I wasn't friendly enough with anyone there to tell them why I wasn't at work and felt so self-conscious that I avoided everyone I could. My face and neck were bruised and I felt pretty terrible, but relieved it was over and I was okay. So I just went everywhere I had to go with a scarf wrapped around me, trying to hide as much as I could. The kids joked that I looked like a hamster with it's cheeks full, as my face was so swollen.

The doctor told me to take co-codamol and other painkillers to keep on top of the pain, and although I did take them, I was also worried because they told me they were extremely addictive and not to be taken for more than three days, unless in extreme circumstances. I wasn't keen, and worried that anything deemed addictive might cause a problem for me. I was already seeing the effects of my addictive or obsessive nature and knew what I was like without introducing anything stronger. And I preferred wine. So I only took the painkillers for a couple of days, preferring to ease off, and take a couple of paracetamol if I had to, looking forward to my usual glasses of wine in the evening. I knew it wasn't the best idea in the world, but I put it out of my mind and carried on like I normally did. Nothing changed, not even if I was ill. The worst of it was probably when I ignored the instructions and washed painkillers down with my wine anyway. I didn't see it as too much of a problem as I didn't think I was doing it that often, I just didn't want to miss out on my wine, and anyway, it was 'only' paracetamol or ibuprofen, nothing stronger. While Lee was away, it didn't seem to matter as I didn't have anyone to hide it from.

CHAPTER 7
2013

Nothing much changed for me over the few years that passed after I got that job. Work was busy, life was busy, we carried on. I finished my degree and got a 2:2. The work had been stressful and hard but for the most part I enjoyed it. I was so proud of myself, but I often look back now and imagine what I would have got if I had given the drink a break for a bit and been more clear headed when I was working! I never did anything in the evening without wine, and that included studying.

One day I was driving home from work when I felt a blinding pain in my head. It hurt a lot and I could barely see. I had to pull over immediately, and wait for a bit for it to clear. I wasn't the sort of person that took time off work or went to the doctors. I didn't like being ill, and I was so self-conscious about drinking that I tried to cover up any complaint that could be drink related. It made me feel sensitive about it and yet it wasn't enough to stop me. It certainly wasn't enough to get in my way and I never wanted to give anyone a reason to tell me not to drink.

Anyway, I assumed the pain in my head was a migraine and once I got home I took some painkillers. It cleared up enough by the evening to mean I was well enough for a drink or two and I assumed that was it. Over the next couple of days it came back, on and off and I kept getting really confused, waiting at the traffic lights one day, I couldn't even work out what the colours were telling me. In the end Alison who I worked with told me to go to the doctor. She noticed that before the migraines came on I struggled to string sentences together properly. It was like I had a little bit of a hole in my memory, it just wasn't there, much as I tried to rummage in my head, certain things just seemed to go. It was terrifying at the time, I felt a little bit like I was losing my mind, but then things went back to normal so I downplayed it and put it out of my mind. It was easier that way. I struggled to face up to things that were so serious, it was so much easier to bury my head in the sand and have a glass of wine to help me relax.

When another migraine hit I eventually did book an appointment. It got to the point that I just wanted to be able to tell everyone I was all right, and to do that I needed the doctor to tell me I was all right. I made light of the symptoms then like I did with most things, but it did worry me. Sitting in the waiting room made me anxious, there was a reason I avoided doctors. Every wall had a warning on it, mostly about alcohol or substance abuse. In between trying to tell myself I was okay I'd convinced myself I was really sick, that I could have something terminal, that drinking was going to kill me. But ignoring it all made it go away for a while. Ignoring it made me feel better. As long as I could avoid situations that didn't remind me that alcohol could be a problem. The posters that talked of addiction scared me. Seeing a poster with symptoms like mine on it made me really worry, and

I would often promise myself I wouldn't drink, to prove myself to myself that I was fine, but of course by the evening I had talked myself back into it, reassuring myself, telling myself that women like me didn't have problems like this. I had no choice though, and there I was sitting, looking at all these warnings and worrying. Then it was my turn. The doctor called me in and asked me to explain my symptoms. She took my blood pressure. Then she looked at me with a serious face and told me I was at high risk of a stroke. I couldn't believe what I was hearing. She repeated it and told me I should go home and rest. I was to come back the next day and have my blood pressure checked again. She told me if it hadn't dropped I would have to go straight to Accident and Emergency. She prescribed me a bag of drugs to take home, one to prevent migraines, one to stop migraines when I got them, one to relax the muscles in my neck as there was a theory that damage I had to my vertebrae from stopping a fight in a classroom years before could be pinching nerves and causing problems too, and some heavy duty painkillers. That trip to the pharmacy cost me a fortune! I took them home, but was scared to take them. I worried that if I could become so dependent on alcohol, which was relatively easy to obtain, just what sort of problems I could get into with a bag full of drugs including diazepam. It was strange too, no one asked at all if I drank, or how much, and as they didn't ask, I didn't offer it.

I went home in a state. Telling me I had to go to A&E only increased my blood pressure and my stress. But of course, I didn't relay it all to my husband, or to anyone else, just certain edited bits. I didn't want to worry him and I certainly didn't want it to affect my ability to open a bottle or two of wine that evening.

So I brushed it off, said it was just a migraine and went on about my day.

I was terrified going back to the doctor the next day. I was so worried that there was something really wrong with me, even more worried that there was something really wrong with me that would mean I would have to stop drinking. The doctor I saw previously wasn't there when I was called back in, it's rare that you can get an appointment at our surgery when you need one, let alone see the same doctor twice. I was called in and had to explain everything again, and the new doctor read through my notes. He told me my blood pressure was okay and he saw no reason for me to have to go to the hospital. He almost seemed surprised that I had been told that in the first place. I was so relieved, but also quite confused. The stress that had caused me, thinking something was seriously wrong had been a lot to think about, it was great to think I was okay, and yet, I didn't really know if I was.

The doctor wanted to delve more into my history and work out what was going on. He took his time and didn't try to rush me. He came to the conclusion that the pain in my head might actually be referred pain from my the damage in my neck. It wasn't unbearable but was affected by the cold, and sometimes the mobility I had there wasn't the best. I hadn't, for a very long time, taken the pain relief I had been prescribed and it was manageable, I had learned to live with it. But he was helpful and being listened to restored a little of the faith I had lost in doctors over the years. He recommended I carry on with the pain relief for a while and the diazepam too. He told me that would help to relax my muscles, especially when I was sleeping which would help keep tension from my neck. He thought that I might have jarred it when driving, which could have caused the pain, the migraines and everything else. Of course, being treated, and being listened to was one thing, but listening to the advice was another. I was nervous of the diazepam, so put it in a drawer, to be there if I had to but preferably not used. The good news on my side, and possibly the only bit I really paid attention to, was the fact that this injury wasn't drink related. Of course, I hadn't divulged how much I drank, and when asked, just said 'a bit' thinking I could brush it off and make it seem normal. For me though, it just meant that I could carry on as I was. That little niggle was there in the back of my mind, just asking if I was drinking too much, but again, I could just brush it off and ignore it. I was referred to the hospital where I had to go for a CT scan which showed one of my nerves was irritated, which from time to time causes a lot of pain and numbness in my arm and hand. Although it is annoying, even to this day, it is a relief to know it is not anything more sinister.

Somewhere in the midst of all this, my sleep began to get quite badly affected. Sometimes in the evening I'd fall asleep due to how much I'd drunk. I'd convince myself it wasn't drink related, but just because I'd had a busy day and was genuinely tired. Even without these evening naps, I'd fall into a pretty heavy sleep straight away, but after an hour or two, I'd wake up. Unable to get back to sleep night after night I got increasingly frustrated and began to look for things to help. Maybe if I'd cut out the wine it would have helped. Instead I started looking at sleeping tablets and found some I could buy over the counter, 'for short term use'. Although they weren't to be taken with alcohol, I kidded myself that they would be okay, at least occasionally. Occasionally didn't last very long though and I was soon taking them every night, but keeping it a secret from everyone. I began to visit different chemists, so that when they warned me they weren't for prolonged use, I could lie and say I didn't use them regularly, without the fear of being caught out. Occasionally when my neck was really bad I swapped one out for a diazepam deludedly thinking I was following the doctors recommendation by taking it to help relax my muscles.

I knew I wasn't behaving responsibly, that I wasn't looking after my body well enough, but I honestly thought I'd be okay. I didn't know what else to do, so I just kept going. In some ways looking back, I wonder whether my use of sleeping tablets actually allowed me to convince myself that my drinking wasn't such a problem. Sometimes when I woke up with a groggy head it was easy to pretend it wasn't wine, especially when I had other things to blame it on. Sleeping tablets were a good reason for the grogginess, and somehow, I told myself that the amount I was drinking wasn't a problem. I'm not sure even now how I did that. I don't know how I could have knowingly drunk quite so much without being more concerned as to how it would affect me. I seemed to think I was immune.

On some level I must have known I was drinking too much, even if I couldn't admit it to myself. At Christmas we had family over, which was unusual, as our two sides of the family weren't close and I always worried that things would go wrong and turn out badly, but Lee and I wanted to try, we wanted to have everyone together, even if it was a little stressful. On this occasion we had both sets of parents, Lee's Aunt, Uncle and Grandad over. It was meant to be lovely, but I did need a couple of glasses of wine to relax. I was on edge until then. Later in the evening Lee came over unwell with a terrible migraine, I think it must have been the stress! But it was unusual for him and so bad, he ended up going to bed. I stayed downstairs and chatted with everyone until they left. We had a nice evening all in all, but later, when I went to bed, I tripped over clothes I think, that Lee had left on the bedroom floor, as I hadn't wanted to turn on the light. In this instance it was an actual accident and not drink related, but stumbling backwards I fell into the chest of drawers and really hurt my back. It hurt for a few days, and although I was sure I had just bruised it, as I did fall pretty hard, I was concerned on the inside that it was my kidneys or my liver, as it was in that area. Of course, I didn't tell anyone that. It made me feel squeamish for days though.

I had paranoia of illnesses too. It began quite innocently, but as time went on, every time I hurt myself I became afraid that there was something seriously wrong with me. Something probably caused by my drinking, that could be stopped if I stopped, but of course I didn't. The more I worried, the more I drank, because while it didn't stop me worrying, it did stop me thinking about it. I'd Google something that I was concerned about and scare myself, turning something fictitious into a constant worry. Drowning my sorrows was the best way I found to cope with anything. It was much easier than trying to talk to anyone about it.

Another thing that I buried my head in the sand with was my tummy. Worry and alcohol mixed together made each other worse, I know that now, looking back, but then I didn't. At least not definitely enough to do something about it. I struggled to eat and I struggled not to drink. As a coping mechanism I began to worry about where toilets were when I was out and about, if it looked like there weren't any or there might be a large queue, and therefore a wait, I wouldn't eat when I was out. It sounds trivial, but coping on a daily basis when you don't want to eat anywhere except for at home can be difficult. I lost weight, but didn't really worry too much as I was happy to fit into smaller clothes. I didn't really think about the long term effects of alcohol on my system, nothing seemed too serious, but to be honest, due to the amount I was drinking, I probably didn't have too much time to think clearly about it either.

In the Autumn I got a chest infection. It didn't go away and eventually I admitted I'd have to go to the doctors again. Try as I might to avoid them, I seemed to be having to go in more often that I would have liked. I tried to explain how my tummy burned, and was prescribed something to stop the acid reflux that they diagnosed. I was told it was because I was coughing so much, but I knew I wasn't, in fact for some reason, although my chest was a problem, I wasn't coughing much at all. This fact was overlooked though and I took the advice I was given coming home, taking the tablets, along with my antibiotics. Firstly, the antibiotics really made my chest feel better, which was a relief, but the other medication multiplied the problems I was having with my tummy, and I felt awful. For several days I tried to get by, until the weekend, when I felt so bad I rang the NHS helpline for advice. Listening to my symptoms, they were understanding, but worried, and made me an appointment for the same day at my local hospital. Had I known they would do that I wouldn't have phoned, but I went, feeling I couldn't do anything else. While I don't like asking for help, I also don't like to waste other people's time. The doctor there was no nonsense but understanding and when I explained I had been feeling like this for sometime, but the medication had made it worse, he suggested I see a specialist at the hospital, and would ask my GP to refer me. He was surprised that I had been coping with my symptoms for so long without seeking further help. I don't think I had put two and two together with the fact that it was drink related, I preferred to push those thoughts from my mind and blame other things. So when he suggested that, it felt like someone was helping. It felt like a relief, and it felt like he was telling me that whatever was wrong with me wasn't my own fault. I came away with another prescription of something to settle my tummy, I was told to stop the medication I was already on, and I was asked to follow up with my GP for more tests. That in itself was nerve-wracking. Surprising myself, I did go to the doctors, and explained everything again. Given that it was some time after I'd seen the doctor at the hospital, I was feeling considerably better, and while not one hundred percent, I presented much better than I had done previously. The doctor didn't seem overly concerned, but ran some blood tests, after asking a few questions. They wanted to check several things, one of them being my liver function and my CRP levels, which made me nervous. While I had admitted I drank alcohol often, I hadn't been honest about how much I drank. I almost didn't want to get the results, I was so worried about them, it was one of the first times I'd been forced to face my habits and the effects they might have on me. I put it off and waited until I could phone the surgery when I was on my own to get the results which from memory was in the supermarket car park on my way home from work, one of the few places I could guarantee I wouldn't be overheard. I waited while the results were looked up and was told that my liver function was of concern, but everything else looked okay. They wanted me to book another appointment to go back in and have them redone, but of course, I put my head back firmly in the sand and didn't go.

CHAPTER 8
2014

So, as you'll guess, I was finding work hard. It wasn't that I couldn't do it, I could and I did it well. It's just I took it home with me too. I found myself thinking more and more about the events of the day, worrying about the children I worked with, and worrying if I was up to the standard expected in the schools I worked with, but it was increasingly hard. Every night involved wine, several glasses just to relax, unwind and stop thinking about what had gone on. I felt like I was on a hamster wheel, everything just rolled from one thing into the next, there was no relief, except when I had a glass of wine. It was stressful and I knew by now I was realistically drinking far too much, especially with my health worries, but by now, I was terrified of admitting it. So I didn't. It was as if, as long as I didn't say it, I could allow myself to carry on ignoring it.

Sometime in the past couple of years my husband and I started up a fused glass business. It was one of the few things I relaxed doing, but even that involved a glass of wine. I'd go down to my workshop when the kids were in bed and relax making glass and drinking wine, usually listening to Zane Lowe on Radio One. It was nice, and as the business grew I started making awards and selling glass to several shops so I was busy. I also went to a lot of shows, and despite the hard work lugging it all around, setting up stands and selling for three days at a time, it was great. It made me think, if I could make it pay, it could take over and become my full time job. It was an exciting time, and I enjoyed having the freedom to work under my own steam with no one to answer to. I began to get asked for more and more commissions too, and so I spent more time down in the workshop. At the time it fitted around work, most of the shows I did were on the weekends, or holidays, I only had to have the occasional Friday off work, and they were good about letting me. I really wanted to push it and make it successful. It meant a lot to me.

At the same time, my husband's situation at work changed. His future had always been secure in his company, and it was thought one day he would take the lead, but then another family member showed an interest and came into the business. Working in a family business when you aren't one of the family is always going to prove tricky, especially when the values they hold are at odds with yours, so things were unsettled for a while. Given that my Lee had often been employing his Dad, who was an electrician, to work for him on a lot of projects, we began to talk about the possibility of setting up our own company. We weren't for want of ideas, but honestly I didn't know how much chance there was of it happening. It's great to have a pipe dream but we didn't have enough savings to do it on our own, so we talked to his Mum and Dad about the possibility of it being the four of us. When he was young, Lee had been expected to go and work with his Dad in their electrical business, but it hadn't happened. He had wanted his own path and now we realised how beneficial that had been for us, he had gained his own sets of skills far different to his Dad's, but bringing the two of them back together now could mean the chance of something great. It was a lot, and my mother and father in law despite all their good points, do have a habit of over-thinking before they do anything. They really take their time, and assess all the possibilities so to be honest, I didn't think there would be a huge chance of anything really happening. I thought for all the talking that was happening, nothing much would change.

I pushed on with the fused glass business, I thought logically, if there was a chance my husband could make his dream work, so could I. I was totally supportive of him, but I did see it as 'his' project. I'd only ever been the wife of the company director before. While I knew what his company did, and enjoyed talking to clients and customers I didn't know any of the technicalities, and I didn't really see it was my place. It was a difficult time. More difficult was when it was decided that we would go ahead with the new business. Lee's Mum and Dad had a nest egg which meant they could fund the start up and the beginning of the new company, but Lee would be an employee (of theirs) for the first time in ages. That was a weird thing to get our heads around, as was knowing for a while money would be tight. It was all in aid of the bigger picture, but being as there was only one pot of money, it made sense to keep as much as we could of it in the business, rather than take it out for our wages. New machinery and other costs were expensive so we needed to be careful if we wanted it to work.

It was the start of a new chapter, a chance to start something great for our family. Lee was keen to be able to say we had tried, and not get to forty and wish we had. It was just a whole other level of pressure. A whole lot of unknown.

The first few months were quiet, it was just my husband then, with his Dad joining him a few days here and there if he didn't have any of his own work on. Then work started to pick up, and Lee didn't want to turn anything away, he wanted to please every customer and really make the company work, which meant he took on more and more, and worked ridiculously long hours, but this time, it was all for us. So I couldn't and didn't complain. Work was still crazy for me and I wanted to be out of there, I didn't realise how much until Lee's Mum asked if I wanted to work for them too. They needed someone in the office, someone to take the customer enquiries and answer the phone so Lee could work on actual projects without quite so many distractions. I was so relieved I cried, when they asked me. I hadn't expected it, not so soon anyway, and I thought it would be okay. I thought I'd be good at it. I could deal with people and that predominantly was what I would be doing now, a whole different industry, but somewhat the same.

In my time working with the children I made a good friend in our groundsman John. He had been a policeman before coming to work with us, and was quite wise. John often came over for a chat, but also could be counted on for an extra pair of hands when we needed it for the safety of the children. He was a calm voice in the storm and it was nice sometimes to have a sounding board from someone who understood. He was always ready to impart advice or guidance when it was needed, of course, I never once spoke to him about my drinking. When I told him I was leaving, he actually told me it was about time, and that he had been worried about me. He told me afterwards he thought I had been on the edge of a nervous breakdown. That was a shock, and of course, me being me, I dismissed it, until a few years later when I looked back and realised it made sense. Looking back now, I see that he probably saw the up and downs of my mood more clearly than I did. Rolling in to work in the mornings, I always had a complacent can do attitude often along with a fuzzy head. I'd do my job, I'd focus on the kids, but once they had gone and the night before had begun to wear off, I would be all over the place again, worrying and fretting about everything and nothing.

John was probably one of the few people I could have talked to but I didn't. I didn't know how to. On the occasions I did try to work up the courage to talk to anyone else, I felt very brushed off. More than once I'd been told to, "pull myself together", as if I could just stop drinking. Those I spoke to couldn't see what a problem I had, and I wonder sometimes if it was harder for some of them because a few seemed to drink a lot too? I never questioned that I was bringing things up for them, but each time I was told to drink less, as if I could, it made me feel I was being silly, or blowing it out of proportion. On the one hand, that attitude, and the brushing off of my feelings made me feel daft for worrying, while on the other hand, it just made me feel that I didn't need to worry. It reinforced my thoughts that I was okay really, despite how much I was drinking.

CHAPTER 9
2015 & 2016

I'm going to call this the slightly blurry years... I've said it before and I'll say it again, but sobriety is hard. Especially for those of use who have had years and years of ingrained use of alcohol in our lives.

So much of our culture involves drinking. It is as normal to expect a drink of wine or beer as it is to expect a cup of tea. So when someone realises that alcohol has become a problem in their lives it isn't just the drinking that has to stop, they also have to entirely relearn the way they live. Coming from a family that always 'enjoyed a drink' I grew up expecting that that was the normal way to relax, that it was okay in the evening to always have a drink with your dinner and more after. It was so normal that I really didn't think for a very long time that I had a problem, and even when I questioned it, I wondered how many people would believe me. I didn't believe myself. I wasn't sure how I could really have a problem, when I didn't drink in the day, even thought it was the first thing I thought of when I woke up. By that I don't mean I wanted to drink first thing in the morning, but I often planned my day to make sure I could drink later on. I honestly thought if I spoke to anyone, they would think I was after attention. I wasn't, trust me, no one in their right mind would put themselves through recovery unless they had to.

But, I was still bumping along, I hadn't hit rock bottom yet. I'd started my new job, expecting to be amazing at it, and that's when things started to come crashing down. Working with family was far, far harder than I ever thought it would be. I can say that now, and know even if they are reading it, that they will agree with me, and yet, we have somehow worked through it, because we still work together now (I'm writing this in 2021). Adding to the family, our eldest son also works with us now as one of our team, so we can't be that bad - he wouldn't put up with us if we were!

I found my confidence take a big hit, suddenly I was in a new job, one I really didn't know anything about and I felt stupid. Lee didn't have the time to train me, or explain everything, and I just muddled through. I could answer the phone, I could talk to the customers, but after that, I wasn't much help and I wanted to be. Coupled with that, my mother in law was doing the accounts. To start with she fitted it around her job as there wasn't too much to do, but as we got busier, she went part time and came into our office more and more, before resigning and coming in full time. It should have been fine, but we butted heads a lot. She had her firm way of doing things and struggled to see my point of view. I believe she thought I was more confident than I was, but I felt every criticism or comment as a personal attack. It was hard, and I began to hate being there. It really affected our relationship for a long time. I felt she would brush over her mistakes, but pick up on mine, and whether that's true or not, it added to my feelings of failure. I felt that my voice had gone, even Lee who had run a company bigger than this before, struggled to get his point across to them sometimes as they had strong ideas on how things should be done. I had to keep reminding myself that if it wasn't for them we wouldn't have been able to even start the business, and that they needed Lee to make it work, but I couldn't really see where I fitted in. It was a difficult time, and I really began to think I had made a mistake, at least in my old job, however stressful it was, I was good at it.

I used to have a friend, (I used to have more than one, but that is another story). Well anyway, her eldest and my youngest at the time were at the same primary school together, which was ten miles or so out of town. Her partner worked weekends and only had Mondays off, so we took in in turns to pick up the boys from school a couple of days a week to give each other a little more time. On a Monday she would pick her son up from my house, not stopping for long because she often had her other half with her, and on a Tuesday after work I'd go to her house. It was nice, I often used to bring Joe and Katie too and my friend had a younger daughter, so the kids all used to play together while we chatted. One day my friend's sister joined us. I didn't know her well, but she seemed nice, and the bonus was instead of being offered tea, I was offered wine instead. This was great and we just settled in, enjoying the evening. One week rolled into the next and we joked, while chatting and sitting out in the sun in the back garden as the kids played again, about 'Tuesday Night Wine Club'. I remember being pleased that I had found a little loophole in my plan, I had an excuse to drink somewhere that wasn't at home, and of course, seeing as it was after 5pm, as soon as I got home, I could carry on drinking. Another glass as I was cooking, another one with dinner, and so one, until bedtime. Any worries I had about my drinking were curtailed because here I was being offered wine by two other mothers, surely that was proof that everyone else drank as much as me? At least on some days? The problem was of course, this was just another friend I couldn't talk to about it, one who I had been close to and ended up withdrawing from, and keeping at arm's length, because the only person I ever spoke to about drinking was Lee and even then it was tricky. If I was feeling vulnerable it was almost easy to admit I had a problem, to ask for help, but I was afraid to, because I knew that the minute I really admitted to it, beyond the wondering and questioning stage, I would actually have to do something about it, and I wasn't ready to do that. In fact, the thought of doing something about it was awful. As much as I resented the hold wine had over me, I also loved it, and in the end it was like saying goodbye to a best friend. A best friend I wanted to kill. The sad thing was that my friend had a relative who was an alcoholic. I knew the person too, and in fact her kids went to school with mine, so my friend probably would have understood much more than I gave her credit for. This person had a very hard time too, but unfortunately for her family, she is no longer with us.

Over the years occasionally, either Lee or myself brought up drinking. He enjoyed a beer, but really could take it or leave it. We'd make a deal to stop, or ease off, to only drink at the weekends, but nothing ever lasted, I couldn't do it. I could maybe last a day, by the skin of my teeth, but it was verging on impossible. By now I was at the point where I would have a glass or two before Lee came home, wash my glass, put it away and pour my 'first' one when he got home. I became a wine ninja in the way I'd refill my glass secretly. If Lee left the room or went upstairs I would be able to down my glass, get to the kitchen to refill it and be back to the sofa before he noticed. At least I kidded myself he didn't notice. I'm sure he must have. I was so envious of his ability not to drink; it was frustrating, and I just didn't understand how he could take it or leave it. I wanted to be like that, and yet I couldn't get to a point where I could be without it.

Things weren't right with me in general now, drinking was beginning to really take its toll, although I still couldn't bring myself to admit it to myself. My nervous tummy was constantly there, it bubbled away and got to the point that eating was almost impossible. I'd be hungry, but put food in front of me and I couldn't eat. I'd lost three stone by the final year of my drinking. I remember picking up a skirt in Next and it hanging off me. I had to go back twice to pick up a smaller size, and was actually pleased at the amount I had lost. I didn't see it at the time either, but when I look back at photos, my head doesn't look the right size for my body and I didn't look well. One night, having worked three days with my glass at a show, I packed up and came home. It was hot, probably the middle of the summer and I hadn't eaten properly all day. I cooked something for us and the kids, Lee was still at work so I made something that would keep for him, but by the time the food was ready, I couldn't eat it. I just sat in the garden in the sun and drank my wine. My liquid diet did wonders for my dress size, but it wrecked my mental health. I couldn't relax at all at this point. Everything was a worry, I couldn't eat out, in fact, I could barely go out, except if I knew exactly what to expect. I became obsessed with knowing where the toilet was, as I often got an upset tummy, due to both my stress levels and my drinking. It was terrible. The more I worried, the worse I got, so the more I drank and around the cycle went on. There was no way out of it. Remembering it now, it was like I couldn't breathe, like I was suffocating under it all, and I didn't know how to help myself. There was no way I could settle myself without wine. It was a really horrible time.

So, in the summer of 2015 I stopped drinking. I cried a lot. Lee was supportive and helped me get through the first couple of days. Funnily enough but even now I remember what day of the week it was because I had to take my daughter to a hospital appointment. It was immensely hard, but I did it, and two days in I felt better than I had in ages. My appetite began to come back, and the anxiety I always felt, the hyper-vigilance causing me to be constantly on edge eased off. I felt so good that I convinced myself that I didn't really have a problem and by the weekend I was confident that I had over-reacted. It didn't help that it was sunny, and as I drove home one evening, I could see people enjoying the sunshine outside pubs with their drinks. It was very tempting, so I had a few myself. Moderation doesn't work for me. I've proved that now on several occasions. Within a very short time I was right back where I had been again, except possibly worse, because now I really knew for sure that it wasn't possibly a problem, it was definitely one.

I found that the trouble with admitting a problem to your loved ones is that it makes you accountable. I was terrified of letting Lee down. I think I had given up on myself at this point, but I hadn't on him. I would try not to drink, but I couldn't imagine life without wine. I couldn't see how I would relax, or how I would reward myself. I was so deluded that I felt I had earned a drink, and I didn't know how to replace it. I had no idea how I would reward myself after any sort of a day and I didn't know how I would be able to switch off in the evenings. There were so many questions that I couldn't answer and so I did what I always did when I had a problem and drank. But like I said I didn't want to let Lee down, and the problem with addiction is that it can make you secretive. So, I tried to hide it. I have never been so conflicted in all my life, and yet the times I had tried to stop drinking just resulted in making me feel like I couldn't give it up, that I wasn't strong enough to do without it. The resentment I had towards wine was growing as I began to realise just how big a hold it had over me, but regardless, every night I still poured a glass or two, or three, or four. I was over the two bottles of wine I used to limit myself to now, and ashamed of the recycling I was putting out each fortnight. I would try to hide it, or take it in the car to the recycling bank, embarrassed that the neighbours would see or hear it being taken away in the morning. My excuse was that the kids enjoyed smashing the glass, and they did, we made a game out of it, but they wouldn't have minded not doing it either.

I hated myself. I felt so weak, and so out of control. It was my rock bottom I guess and that was where my love of drinking stopped, when I woke up and realised it controlled me, that it wasn't a release, or an excuse for relaxation anymore. It was a tie, an anchor almost, something that held me back, and controlled the way I thought and behaved. It was the scariest thing I have ever done, but admitting my problem and learning to confront it saved my life. It changed me as a person, or maybe it didn't, instead maybe it gave me back the person I was before all the drinking. It wasn't easy, trying and slipping up and trying again, each slip up made me feel weaker and the hold drink had on me felt stronger, but now each day is easier.

I found it hard to talk to people about drinking, or not drinking in my case. I wasn't sure whether talking would help or not, and much as I wanted others to talk to me, once I had broached the subject, they didn't. Now I know they must have found it difficult too, but if not dealt with, it can become the elephant in the room. I avoided people for a long time in my early months of sobriety, to some extent I still avoid people now. I found everything challenging and some days are harder than others. People didn't get how hard it was for me, and although I'm not expecting them to, sometimes a little understanding goes a long way. However, if you're the one giving up you do need to remember if they aren't going through the same thing, how can they really get it?

In the Autumn we had a big project for work come up in London. Lee often travelled, and this time had been asked to design and manufacture some giant poppies to be put up in Waterloo Station for Remembrance Day. Lee had a meeting before the install to run through some final details before the install and asked if I'd like to go with him. Although the idea made me nervous I decided to go, as I was trying to push myself a little more than normal out of my comfort zone. It would have been easier to stay at home; I would have been able to have an extra glass of wine or two the night before. I probably had plenty anyway, but I think I was trying to drink a little less because of the early start. We went up in the morning early, and ate breakfast on the way, before going to meet the client. After the meeting, Lee took me to Hatton Garden and we had a lovely time walking round and looking at diamonds. It was quite an eye opener looking at how expensive some of the jewellery was, with all the security men walking up and down the street keeping an eye on what was going on. It wasn't long after the Hatton Garden Heist, so security was much heavier than normal. I'd never had to be let into a jewellery shop before and locked in before, but it was a great experience and lovely to spend time for just the two of us. The kids were with their grandparents so although we were doing the trip in the day, we didn't have to rush to get back and Lee suggested stopping for dinner. We thought we'd get out of the city first and back to the car, but it wasn't until we were back on the motorway that I realised how hard it would be to find somewhere nice to stop without knowing exactly where we were going. We were quite hungry by this time and so wondered if we should just stop at a service station. Normally that would be fine for me, especially in the day, but in the evening it meant that I couldn't have a glass of wine, and despite the fact that I was supposed to be cutting down, I was beginning to get really twitchy about not having a drink. I knew that if we went home, it would be too late, and I wouldn't get one there. I hated feeling like it, and wanted to cover it up, even though Lee must have known, I felt that I was being clever, hiding my need for a drink and covering it with something else. I was pretty naive I must say. Lee had told me once or twice of a chain of restaurants he liked to stop at when he travelled so I decided we had to find one to go to on the way home. It was well out of the way, and must have been quite a detour for us, but Lee still went there and didn't say a word. At least he didn't until I asked for a glass of wine. I tried really hard to make it last, but it just wasn't quite enough like usual, and I had to have one more. It made me feel so much better, and I remember being surprised that Lee was upset with me, disappointed at me even. He didn't say much until after, but the mood changed and I just knew I shouldn't have had a drink, but I needed it. It was another one of those confusing times, when I hated the thing that made me feel better. I wanted to be one of the women who enjoyed a glass of wine, and whose husbands laughed and smiled indulgently, but of course, for me, those days were long gone.

A few weeks later, Lee took the team up to install the poppy display. It was a big job and due to it being on Waterloo Station, they needed to do it overnight, and be clear for the rush hour the next morning. They left in the afternoon, and having the kids, and therefore not able to help, I stayed at the office before going home. It wasn't until later that evening that I had a call from Lee saying they had forgotten something. It wasn't a big thing, but it was something needed for the display and as they had taken two vans, it wasn't realised it was missing until they had started the install as each thought it was in the other van. We needed to get it to them as soon as we could so I managed to get hold of my mother in law who went back to work, collected the item and packaged it up while I got hold of a courier to organise a speedy delivery to the station before everyone left again. It was a bit of a nightmare, but I managed it. The next thing was getting the package to the courier. Of course, it was after 6pm so I had already had at least one glass of wine, but I was aware that my mother in law didn't like driving at night, which caused a problem. I needed to get the package collected and taken twenty miles to the depot, before 8pm or it wouldn't be delivered in time. I didn't drive once I had a drink though. I never did. It was one of my sticking points, and so I couldn't go out, but I also couldn't tell my mother in law why I couldn't drive. I was lucky though and she offered without much persuasion, thinking it would be best for me not to drag the children out in the evening. I was so relieved not to have to make another excuse for why I couldn't go out, and I managed to get the parcel to the team in time. So once again, things managed to work out, which meant another day went by when I could avoid my problem.

Things seemed to be coming to a head, although I was still functioning and outwardly not affecting my life generally, my drinking was causing more and more problems. It was becoming more important than other things and causing arguments. So, in the winter of 2015 I tried again to stop completely. Again I failed. And again I got worse because the thing is, one glass of wine is not enough for me, and that one glass that I couldn't resist always made everything come tumbling back down. I knew I had to do something serious. I knew I couldn't do it on my own and I knew I couldn't go on the way I was. I didn't like myself anymore. Every day was a battle and I'd learned that I could not moderate my drinking at all. I grew to resent the wine I loved so much, I hated the hold it had over me, and yet I just couldn't say no to it. More than once I smashed a glass, literally throwing it across the room in frustration because I didn't want it and yet I needed it. I had never been so conflicted in my life, and the fact that I wanted and at the same time didn't want something so much just confused me more than anything. I felt so much shame and I was resentful towards myself because I didn't feel like I had any control.

We decided to take the kids ice skating just before Christmas as there was a pop up ice rink in our local town centre. I'd wanted to keep it just to us and the kids but then we thought of inviting my in-laws. That was fine, they might not have completely understood, but they were trying so I didn't mind too much. Unfortunately that then changed as someone we knew overheard us talking and rather than brushing it off, my mother in law then invited them too. That upset me, it wasn't what I wanted and suddenly it became a bigger thing than I had anticipated. It was just meant to be quiet. It was enough to make me want to stay at home, but I was worried I would have looked rude. I cared too much then about what other people thought, and I should have followed my instincts or at least told the other people that it was meant to be family only. Protecting myself might seem selfish to some, but then it was what I needed. Nowadays, I have learned that on occasion my feelings need to come first but I generally don't like to cause upset, so I just went along with it. The problem was, the other people that came were totally insensitive to my situation, and while we were thinking about getting hot chocolate, they went to the beer tent. It was really early days for me and although I never had a problem with beer that really made me wobble. Lee and I just went into Costa, as it was the only place you couldn't see the beer tent and people weren't drinking. Actually we didn't just go, I practically ran there to hide. We still had a lovely time with the kids, but it was much harder than I had envisaged it. That evening I just went home and cried. Lee held me and said all the right things, but I just didn't know what to do with myself. It wasn't just unexpectedly being faced with alcohol on an evening out, it was more that it was also a Saturday, a day of the week when before I didn't need an excuse to drink in the evening. The day of the week that wherever you were, it was meant to be okay to drink, and I couldn't. Being out and coming home to not drinking was strange and hard to deal with. I felt like I was missing out. Being confronted with other people drinking just reminded me that I couldn't, and at that point, it felt very much that I was losing something rather than gaining my life back. I couldn't focus, I couldn't watch the TV, I couldn't do anything. Without that wine, I felt like I'd lost my purpose. What was the point, if I couldn't get through the day and have the reward I was looking for? Nothing seemed like it would ever be 'right' again, I felt lost and muddled by everything. I hated feeling the way I did, but I didn't know what to do to pull myself out of it.

During my second attempt (and failure) at sobriety, I finally faced up to the fact I might need to ask for help. I hid in my workshop at the bottom of the garden (where I used to make fused glass in my previous life) and phoned a helpline. Months before on one of my trips to the doctor I had picked up a leaflet for Addaction. I'd hid it away, embarrassed that I had it, unable to phone the number and yet also unable to throw it away. When I finally phoned, I wasn't sure what I was expecting, but I was terrified that someone somewhere would assume I was a bad mother and try to take my kids away. That they'd only see the bad bits of me and none of the good. While I sometimes might have been shorter of patience than I would have liked, I knew that I had never put them in danger and I still never drank in the day or took unnecessary risks, I just didn't know if the people on the end of the phone would believe that. I was still under the illusion that alcoholics were somehow different to me, people that had lost everything and no longer cared. I couldn't quite align myself with what I thought the definition of an alcoholic was.

I was a mess during the call. I spoke to someone who listened, reassured me, asked me a few questions that were more about my safety, and those who lived with me, before putting me on a waiting list to speak to a someone else. I didn't hear anything for three months, and felt forgotten. It felt like I wasn't good enough, like they didn't want to help me and in that time my strength and resolve slipped and I had started drinking again. I could never manage more than a few days or a week, but it always felt like the longest time ever. Finally someone called me back and I had someone to offer me help, but they had no answers, just a lot of questions for me. They suggested I come in and meet the team and speak to a counsellor. I was assigned a key worker who I will call Bill. Bill listened when we met, but he didn't have answers either. Except to tell me not to stop drinking. I thought he was joking, but I had heard right. I was drinking so much that actually stopping could have been really bad for me. It was frustrating. At this point all I wanted was to stop drinking and suddenly I was being told to carry on. It was so hard I couldn't seem to do it on my own and yet no one seemed able to help me. It was so confusing. Bill told me to cut down, but only by about half a glass each week. He said it had to be manageable so I could maintain it and not slip back. I already knew what it was like to slip, but man, drinking when I wanted to stop was weird and went against everything I had thought.

After our initial meeting I was scheduled to see Bill once a week to keep up to date with my progress. During one meeting Bill suggested I had two ways to go. Either I did all the work myself or I book in for a residential detox. Having tried and failed to give up on my own I really liked the idea of the 'easy' way out so I booked the detox. The idea is that you go into the hospital for a week and with medical intervention come off the substance you are dependent on. I loved the idea of waking up no longer needing or wanting to drink. It wasn't quite so straightforward as that as Bill insisted I needed to have things in place for afterwards, as otherwise it would be too easy to slip straight back to where I had been before. I needed to change my habits in my day to day life to help me stay sober. I was okay with that, but the problem was the waiting list was long and I was done with drinking, I loved it, I hated it, it was confusing, but most of all, I hated the control it had over me.

I don't think Bill and I clicked. I'm assuming he was once an alcoholic, going by his job in an advisory role, but I just don't think he got me, and most of all I wanted to be understood. He never divulged anything, so I didn't know if he understood what I meant or not. When I asked, he just threw things back to me, the only glimmer I got of him as a person was when he told me that there was no way he could have drunk the amount I did because he would be on the floor. While I think he meant it as almost encouragement to moving on, it just felt like another judgement. I didn't feel like our meetings were going anywhere and most of all I was still drinking, which wasn't the point at all. I think he must have understood how I felt, and offered me a place at a small local group meeting. Hoping this would help more I immediately said yes. They were quite close to where I lived, which made me worry a lot but I had no choice. After the second meeting I stopped outside to chat with another group member and someone I knew drove past. They definitely saw me as they waved and I felt like I had a neon sign above me pointing out I was an alcoholic, I felt so self-conscious! I'm sure in reality, they had no idea what I was up to that morning.

The first meeting was strange. It was in a building almost in the centre of town. There were no signs, which I understand, but it makes it hard to know where you're going when it isn't advertised, and I was already on edge. I was early and met by two women who were cagey about why they were there, they clearly didn't want to give away what the group was if I wasn't supposed to be attending. Given the circumstances, I was also cagey about why I was there, so trying to work out if I was in the right place was weird. Finally it was decided that I was and gradually other people came in. The first thing I noticed that all the other attendees had the support of their counsellors, even if they weren't there for the whole session, they just popped in to show their support. Bill didn't. I didn't even necessarily want him to, but again, it just felt like something else I had done wrong, he didn't like me and want to make sure I was okay so it must be my fault. It really upset me to be honest, and yet it was also nice to be in a group with these two ladies. They got it. They understood how it felt, and the best thing for me was when one of the two admitted she was an alcoholic too. I'm not sure if she was advised not to say, she seemed almost like she spoke out of turn, and yet you could feel the room let out a breath when she did tell us. It meant recovery was possible, that people like us could turn back into 'normal' people. It was a relief to see in reality what we could become again.

Obviously I'm not going to disclose anything to identify my fellow anonymous attendees but it's fair to say that it was a diverse group. I connected most with another lady who although older than me was in the same position as me. She knew she had a problem but buried her head in the sand too, finally admitting she had a problem when she had to leave a theme park she was at with her children to buy a bottle of wine which she then sneaked back in with her. A newcomer to the country worked long shifts and not knowing anyone well enough to socialise with, drank to oblivion during their time off. There was another person, who had been in and out of prison during their drug and alcohol addiction. They had been clean until they were stabbed by their partner, but coming out of hospital to find the partner had been arrested and the relationship unreconcilable had been too much, and the familiarity of drugs and alcohol had beckoned.

There were of course other people there in the meetings, and I had nothing and yet everything in common with them. Some people looked at me strangely before I spoke, trying to work out why I was there, like I said, I presented a very together image, as long as I knew there would be wine at the end of the day, and at that point there still was. That made it worse, knowing I was still drinking was just compounding the confusion I felt, and I felt in some ways like a fraud. Going to the meetings was good though, it gave me a connection with others who didn't judge, who didn't just tell me to stop drinking like it was a bad habit. Most of all they understood the ups and downs of addiction, the confusion that it brought, both loving and hating something at the same time.

Something else that came from my meetings was talking with my new acquaintances. Some of them had been through the process more than once, while others also had experiences of their friends to draw on. We shared different ways of coping, and also things that didn't work. Like me, one lady was so used to her wine glass, that instead of replacing it, she filled it with milk, and drank that instead, trying to wean herself off slowly. One of group was really supportive, despite being in a situation far worse than me, having no money for heating and little for food. No one was willing to help them though, as it was a concern that the money would be spent on substances instead. They suggested while I wait for my detox appointment that I could look into a drug that I could take to dissuade me from drinking, I had no idea there was such a thing available. Or rather, I did, but I didn't think it was something that would be available to me. So I made an appointment and saw the doctor.

I still wasn't particularly trusting of doctors; I didn't think they'd believe me or understand. I was afraid they'd tell me just to stop, although I knew full well that wasn't an option for me. I made an appointment at our surgery, but as my doctor wasn't available, I was given an appointment for a new GP. For the first time in a very long time, I felt listened to by a health professional. I didn't have to persuade her, and she believed me when I told her the difficulties I was having. She told me she had worked in addiction wards in a hospital where patients had tried to drink the hand sanitiser for the alcohol in them. While she hadn't to my knowledge been affected by addiction herself, she understood how bad things could get and she didn't judge me. I couldn't imagine ever being in a situation where I'd be that low, but to be understood was such a relief. She prescribed me Antabuse but told me not to take it straight away. I had to get my drinking right down and then I could start the course. The idea is that Antabuse heightens your sensitivity to alcohol and makes you physically ill if you take the tablets and still drink. The idea of it scared me, but it gave me back the control I had lost. If I chose to take the tablets, then I was choosing to try to put a stop to my drinking. I went home after the appointment and told Lee all about it, putting the pot on top of the fridge, making a plan to get my consumption down. It was a strange thing to think I had them, but couldn't take them yet. One night I reached the end of my tether, I think from memory I lasted about two or three days before I had enough, certainly not the weeks I had been advised. I smashed my glass and tipped the last of my wine down the drain. It was like I was possessed; I was so angry with wine and myself for getting into such a mess. Finally I was angry enough to do something about it. So having got rid of my safety net, I took a tablet. My husband watching me in shock just said, "Bloody hell Clu." (Clu is his nickname for me). I think he was pretty shocked that I was finally making a stand. It might not have been the end, but in that moment I think I took the biggest step forward in my recovery. Nothing happened immediately though. I sat there for a minute waiting to feel different or for something to change, but nothing did. I wasn't magically fixed, but, and this is the huge thing, I was finally on the right path.

I created myself a chart back then. It makes me smile now to think about it, but I wanted a visual guide as to how much I was drinking. It was all well and good knowing, but I wanted to scare myself into drinking less if that makes sense. On my computer I made a graph, it had all the days of each month on it and I put the units of alcohol up the side. The idea was that I would be able to mark off each day, hopefully showing as it got lower and lower. I also marked on there the recommended limit of alcohol for the day, just so I could see it. I had taken it with me to the doctor, and showed her too, and while it may not have stopped me drinking, it did provide a really good visual aid and helped me along my way. It was an eye opener to see that I was drinking over the government guidelines of weekly units of alcohol every single day at the height of my drinking and for a long time before. Even when cutting down I was way, way too high. When you look at it like that it is pretty scary to see.

I decided at that point that I wouldn't go back and see Bill. I think it's really important to meet the right person if you're going start picking apart important and personal things. Bill and I didn't suit each other and perhaps I should have asked if there was someone else to see instead of persevering with someone I didn't see eye to eye with. I'd also gone off the idea of the detox, the idea of being away from each other for a week didn't sit well with me or Lee, and I was beginning to think it wouldn't be the quick fix I had hoped. It wouldn't change the way I was wired and the habits I had formed at home, I still had to do that myself anyway. I did finish the meetings though, they stopped after a while, because they couldn't use the venue any longer, and the nearest one from that was ten miles away. So for a while there was nothing that fit me properly, but without each of those things independently, even for a small time, I wouldn't have been able to make the progress I did. Just knowing I had the safety net of the detox was helpful, but I was almost expecting a magic wand to be waved, and of course no one can do that for you.

With the effort Lee was putting into work I began to feel more and more lonely. I felt isolated and although Lee was really patient with me, we began to argue. I can't have been at all easy for him to live with, and I'm grateful to this day that he put up with me. I knew work was important, I knew he had to put the time in, if it was ever going to work for us, but that didn't make it any easier. It sounds so selfish but I was jealous that his company was working out, when mine wasn't. But mine couldn't with the time I put in.

Realistically if I wanted it to be a full time job, I should have been putting in full time hours and I couldn't with work and the kids. So I closed it down. I still have my workshop, but I don't like to go down there. It reminds me of drinking too much. Happy, sunny evenings with a glass of wine, and of course, that isn't me anymore. I'd try to talk to Lee about how I felt, but I needed a drink to be honest, and he felt that by the time I had a drink I was already drunk and rambling. Which I possibly was. I wouldn't have been able to make my point as concisely as I could without the wine. It was hard because I took things so personally, and whenever I had a complaint, he felt I wasn't being tolerant of his parents. It was hard to explain how low I was feeling without it seeming like just a list of complaints. I began to resent work, the commitment he had to put in, the control it had over us, everything. I felt trapped. I didn't know what I was doing and I didn't feel useful, people thought I was more confident and self-assured than I was and yet every comment felt like a personal criticism. I wasn't sure what I could offer to the business and yet, I couldn't leave. If I did it was like a personal rebuke to our family business and despite my feelings, I didn't want to let our family down. A difficult situation arose and with some things being blown out of proportion, my anxious mind just circled on everything, spinning it round and round and making everything ten times worse. So I drank and things got worse. And eventually that was it. I walked out of work one day after having an argument with my mother in law and didn't go back for a few weeks. I remember sleeping a lot. I don't remember much else at all, it's a fuzzy blur that has probably been packed away in the darkest corner of my mind, and that's where I'd like it to stay. On paper I would say I had a breakdown, but of course, with my history of doctors, I didn't go to see one. It would have been one step too far. Explaining how I felt to Lee was one thing but to other people was something else, and I was exhausted. I just didn't want to do anything. No, it was more than that, I couldn't actually do anything. It was all I could do to function on a basic level. Anything unnecessary was too much for me. I was broken. I was worried that we were broken too. Lee and I talked a lot then. We tried to work through the way I was feeling, the way he was feeling. It was hard. My drinking had damaged so much, but most importantly he was (and still is) there.

Lee was so supportive, he tried so many ways to try to help me. He was always there to talk to when I needed him, he'd phone me to check I was okay when he was at work, and more than once he came flying home, a distance of over twenty miles if I didn't answer the phone when he called me. I know I must have worried him a lot. Gradually we started to do more and he'd take me out to nice cafes for lunch. Places that had nice food and nice tea, but no alcohol to worry about. He tried so hard to make it special, and it was. I just struggled to relax with my chaotic mind, as much as I tried, it just wouldn't turn off. We went shopping for nice tea pots, and bought a set that I could save for the evening, to make a bit of a ritual of tea making, rather than go to the fridge for a bottle as was customary. It was nice to have nice things. He bought me face creams and towels, and reminded me that I should be looking after myself. My neck was still causing me problems, and he researched pressure points that he could work on to try to relieve it. He loved me far more than I loved myself. Looking back it makes me feel so sad, that I was like that, I appreciated it all, but it was so hard, such a hard battle to fight and to lose. I felt so alone in my thinking, and it was frustrating because I still felt like I was missing out, that I was losing something and that I was different from other people.

Of course as you may have guessed, I slipped up one more time. During the summer that followed I stupidly thought again that I could moderate. And I could, for a very short time. It was such a relief to be able to have a drink again and I was so careful, one glass of wine was enough. Except it wasn't, it made me grouchy, and I was always on edge, watching what I was drinking and wondering if it was okay, justifying it to myself. That slope is slippery and of course it wasn't long before I was back exactly where I had been before. Just with a bit more self-loathing. It was the year we went to Scotland on a whim one night for a holiday we hadn't planned, and drove the whole length of the country through the night. I was panicking then when I did things out of the ordinary, I was a nervous passenger, having panic attacks and jumping at everything. I think Lee suggested going that evening because we'd had dinner and I'd had a couple of glasses of wine, so I was more relaxed. It seemed like a good idea and we just went, both having the same week off work, and the kids being on school holiday, nothing was in our way. We just threw the camping gear and the dog in the van and went. I wanted things to change, I wanted to be a normal woman who didn't need anything else to keep me sane, but I couldn't do it. I felt so weak. We had a lovely time, I loved being out in nature, away from home and work, but every day had to involve a trip to the shop to stock up on wine. Of course I thought I was hiding it so well, having said I could moderate, I only ever bought a few bottles to last a couple of days, that just never happened, and the next day I would be going back to the shop again. One day we climbed Ben Nevis, it took us nine hours with the kids and it was very cold, but so amazing to do it. Once we were down, although aching, I made everyone go to the supermarket for wine and dinner before we could go back to the tent and relax properly.

We stopped at Blackpool on the way home, taking the kids to the amusements, and it was easier, when we stopped for food I could have a glass of wine with my dinner. I never felt truly relaxed until I was home though, or in this case, back in the tent, with a few more glasses inside me. It was a sad way to be and I hated it. On one day we stopped for lunch, getting a table outside the pub in the sunshine. There was plenty to see as we sat there and the dog was hiding under the table from the sun. It was so hot; we weren't the only ones lingering there for shade for the dogs. We occasionally switched seats to stop ourselves burning too much and eventually Lee decided to take the dog away to find more shade. He left the kids with me and told me to wait, and he'd be back. It was probably the most relaxed I'd been all holiday, just sitting in the sunshine with a glass of wine and the kids.

During this time I began to investigate 'quit-lit' a form of books inspiring sobriety and recovery. A fairly new niche at the time, it seemed that more and more people were beginning to speak up about their struggles with alcohol, and funnily enough, a lot of them were married, working, parents too. It was inspiring to read the stories of others, the way that people like me had overcome their dependencies and gone on to live normal lives. I devoured everything I could like it, I joined online support groups and I tried to connect with other people who were similar to me. But I couldn't quite face up to what I was. I joined groups with a fake name. I hid the books I was reading from everyone including Lee. I felt embarrassed and outed by them, like they were a giveaway, when my drinking really was enough of one in itself. More often though, I found that reading confused me. I read a book by Lucy Rocca, the founder of Soberistas, and her tales of how alcohol affected her, made me feel like I wasn't alone - it was like she was describing me throughout much of her book, with the excessive drinking no matter what the outcome and the lack of ability to stop drinking. I was in awe of her and yet in the back of my mind was a little voice saying how can she be that honest? Why isn't she embarrassed? How can she? I couldn't decide where to align myself because I didn't know quite who I was. On the one hand I was amazed that she had the courage to be so brutally honest, and on the other hand writers like her inspired me. Their honesty was shocking, but so were my secrets.

Whenever I read anything where people had given up completely, it seemed a little removed from me and my life. I still couldn't quite see how it was possible. I don't think I ever thought of this alcohol free thing as being forever. That was far too scary, even though I'd admitted to myself I didn't want to drink any more. Even though I wanted more than anything to be free of the hold wine had on me, I still couldn't imagine a life without it, and thought that maybe if I could get drinking under control, I might be able to have the odd one here and there. Without wine I couldn't see what I'd do, how I'd relax, so I tried not to imagine life like that. I just tried to focus on each moment. Getting through a moment meant I was doing something and gradually those moments built up. However much I didn't want to drink anymore, I wasn't sure what I would do with my time, how I would reward myself in the evenings or relax. I wanted to understand how other people did it, and I wanted to do it to, but alcohol was such a big part of my life, I didn't know how to do it. More to the point, once I'd done it for a bit, I didn't know how to keep doing it.

I'd always loved reading, but in the last few years, had neither the time or inclination to read like I had used to. Even when I enjoyed a book, I struggled to remember what I had read, so missed bits or had to re-read. There seemed little point. With my new alcohol free mind, I re-found my love of reading and started to read anything and everything about alcohol addiction, anxiety, mental-health and loads of self-help books. I could probably open my own library. I began to understand that my addiction was only part of my problem and my mental health needed a fair bit of attention too. I felt pretty low, for letting myself get into such a state, and for not being able to fix it more easily. To be honest, I thought for a long time that if I admitted my problem, people wouldn't believe me, and because of the way I presented myself to the world, they'd just think I was attention seeking. Everything I thought I knew about myself had changed. The 'fun' me wasn't there anymore, just this nervous wreck who was scared of her own shadow. I felt awful about everything I could remember doing, and worse about the things I had forgotten. I had a lot of time on my hands, but no concentration to focus on anything. I wanted to get better, but I didn't know how. I thought by removing wine, everything would be okay. I guess what I hadn't thought about was how long it took me to get there, how many nights and days, so it was of course not going to be a quick fix.

Then one day, I found a blog. It wasn't about addiction, it was just a woman, writing about her imperfect life. She was quite new back then but has gone on to release several books and do some amazing charity work. Constance Hall wrote about the good, the bad and everything in between. She challenged women to rethink the way they thought about themselves and about others. Conversations followed her posts and I began to realise that other people out there struggled too, that no-one had a perfect life and that I didn't need to hate myself for my imperfections. She called her readers 'Queens' and reminded us that it is okay for your crown to slip once in a while. You can always straighten it up again.

It made me realise how vital connecting with other people is to recovery or any sort of mental health difficulty. Actually more than that, I think connections are vital to life. I know there is a lot of negativity surrounding social media, but for me, I found myself self-isolating for a very long time before Covid-19 was a thing. I didn't want to meet people, but talking in the safety of my own home, via my iPhone or computer made it easier. If it hadn't been for being able to make connections with like minded people on platforms like that, I'm not sure I would be where I am now. Even my running club is an online group. I run alone, don't go to club nights but when I want to chat, there are a whole herd of runners there for me. Joining 'real' people in the real world would have been far too much for me at the time and in a lot of ways, even now I prefer to be just that little bit removed. It makes me feel safer.

Lee and I had always talked about having another baby. Neither of us had ever wanted a huge family, but we felt we weren't quite complete yet. The time though had never been right, and with work being so hectic it wouldn't have worked for us. The closeness of age between our children also meant that while three was a handful, four wouldn't have been sensible, so we kept things as they were. The kids got older, and the gap would have been too big, they were each two years apart, so to have a big gap might have been strange. And yet, it always felt like I was missing something. Lee was concerned about my drinking, and I told him I would stop. I don't know how, I just knew I could. It's a strange thing to admit, knowing the amount I drank, but I knew that I wouldn't drink if I was pregnant, I never had before and it mattered more that I protect a baby than myself if that makes sense. I hadn't stopped drinking though, I just cut down, and the more I did, the more I hated it. I didn't even know that was possible, and yet it was. I hated it and yet I still drank it. It was getting boring and I couldn't quite seem to kick it.

I found out I was pregnant with our littlest man on 8th September 2016. Maybe he saved me because I had my last drink on 7th September 2016. I have read so many experiences when people say that they have a baby and it solves everything, or they have a baby to solve everything. It wasn't like that for me, I wanted this baby so very much and had done for a very long time, but it was a very stressful time for me. I worried a lot that my drinking would somehow have affected him, even though I didn't drink at all once I knew I was pregnant. I worried that there might be something wrong with him, a sort of karma for the way I had behaved, and going to the first scan was terrifying. But I shouldn't have worried. Everything was as it should be. The scans were so much more detailed than they had been with the other children, technology has advanced so much! It was so reassuring to see his little fingers and toes counted out, and to see that he was perfectly formed. It didn't stop me worrying, but it did make me feel better.

It seems like recovery should be the end of a journey, the end of a love affair with alcohol that has to end but yet for me it was very much the beginning. In fact, I'd look at it more like chapters, I finished the drinking chapter and began the recovery chapter, and in some ways, although I don't drink any more, I'm still in it. A chapter that lasts years is long, but so was the chapter that led up to my addiction. Unpicking everything takes time and I wasn't that well prepared for that, I didn't realise how much wine was holding me together in a dysfunctional way, but now without it, I am a better person, I know that now.

It was such an achievement to have stopped drinking, but given that it was in September, it did mean that I only had three months of sobriety under my belt by the time Christmas came around. As anyone who has stopped drinking before knows, three months is barely anything. Certainly not enough to learn to rethink all the brainwashing we have coming at us constantly from TV and elsewhere regarding the fun we will have once we have a drink in our hands. I'd got to three months once before and that was where it ended. Although it was the first time I had been this dedicated to it. This year I approached Christmas with trepidation, the year before had been much worse and ended in arguments on the day which was sad. It certainly overshadowed things for my whole family that year. Things we would normally do couldn't be done, like the work Christmas party which was always a good excuse for me to have a few drinks, and normally the free bar that was put on really helped. Even family gatherings had a different feel, as more often than not, they all involved us having a 'nice' few drinks to relax and enjoy ourselves. Our family often travels a fair distance to see one another (several hundred miles) so once there it was often seen a reward to have a drink after the long journey. It was easier to avoid it all. At home though it was no different and my husband and I would often have several glasses of wine or beers throughout the afternoon and evening. It was an excuse to drink earlier, to be allowed to and to enjoy it. I couldn't see how Christmas would be the same without it. That makes me feel quite sad now, but I think the belief that alcohol is so needed and used as a reward by society makes it very difficult to imagine life without it when you have got yourself caught up in a situation like I was.

The year before on Christmas Day itself we had a quiet family day, just my husband and I and the kids. It was lovely, except during Christmas dinner, when I had a bit of a meltdown. I was so angry! I was angry with myself for wanting a drink, angry that I couldn't have one, angry that I didn't want to give in and let myself have one, angry that it was so ingrained that I should have one. Addiction is so confusing. I was frustrated that I couldn't have a drink, just one, when other people could, but of course, that was always my failing, one was never enough, and that was why I ended up drinking again. This year was different. Although I still missed drinking, it wasn't just for me that I was giving up now, it was for the baby, and much as I wanted to never drink again, I also couldn't see how that would work or be possible. I tried to put it out of my mind as much as possible and just concentrate on getting through one day at a time, to think of anything more seemed too much. It was a completely different way of thinking, for me especially when I had been drinking for so many years. I cocooned myself for a long time, I felt safer and happier at home. There was probably an element of nesting but also, I just didn't want to put any extra pressure on myself. I tried to remember what I had been told in my early recovery, to just be kind to myself. It wasn't easy, but it was all I could do.

A few years before, my Christmas party season looked very different to what it does now. I always went out to shop for at least one 'nice' party dress and shoes. I knew I always had at least two parties to go to where I'd wear them, as both my own work threw a party and my husband's work also did, and that was just the events we 'had' to do. They were often quite different evenings, my husband's would always be a bit more of a formal do, normally at a nice hotel, so we'd get a room and make a weekend of it. There was always a free bar too, so that was nice. Of course, that probably wasn't a good thing for me, I didn't need much encouragement. My own work parties were often more quirky. We sometimes had nice meals out at restaurants and hotels, but the one year that sticks in my memory most (I'm not sure how) is the one where the school I worked at put on a James Bond themed evening. We closed off the school library for over a week while it was transformed into a casino. I'm not sure where the money in the budget came from, but it was fully decorated and themed throughout. All the staff arrived dressed as characters from the films and the catering staff put on a great meal, although I don't remember eating it. I do remember making mojitos which I hadn't drunk before and drinking a lot of wine too.

I remember forgetting what I was saying mid-way through a conversation with the deputy head and her husband which was embarrassing. I remember doing karaoke (badly) with some other Bond girls. I remember a big bonfire (I didn't start it!) in the school grounds where I burned my finger and I remember falling asleep on a sofa. I was woken up by someone I worked with who ignored my protests that I was fine and drove me home. And that was all way before I even thought I had a problem and drinking was still 'fun'!

CHAPTER 10
2017

I'd like that to be the end of the story. I'd love it to be that easy... on that day in September I had my last ever drink, the end. But of course that never happens does it? I mean in some ways it is, it's 2021 and I still haven't had a drink, but that doesn't mean that sometimes I haven't wanted one. It took me probably a decade to get into the situation I was in, so it's realistic to think it might take that long to come out of it on the other side. I'm not sure. I know that everyone is different and for me I'm still working on it.

It had been a long time since I had been pregnant. Twelve years in fact! I'd had three perfectly healthy babies before and thought that was what it would be like this time. However, nature had different plans for me. My mental health was not great. That's probably an understatement. I was okay on the outside, like normal, but inside I felt like I was coming apart at the scenes. I couldn't do anything without worrying. In fact everything I did was surrounded with worry and overthinking. It was a very difficult time. After one routine appointment with the midwife I panicked on the walk home. I felt like everyone was watching me, and I began to walk faster. Of course the panic increased and I pretty much ran home, only slowing down once I had the front door shut behind me. It was awful and I know, unrealistic, but my anxieties often are, and come out of the blue. I cried once I was indoors, but it took me a long time to calm down and ended up curling up in bed for the afternoon.

I was terrified of the scans. At a time when I should have been so excited, I was worried that I had caused a problem to my baby, that it would be my fault and he would be deformed or worse. I had found out extremely early that I was pregnant and hadn't had a drink since, but the worry was still there. At the first scan it was amazing to see him looking healthy and whole. The scans had come on so much since we had the other three children and the detail was amazing. They counted fingers and toes and even checked for cleft palate. It was unbelievable and he was okay. I counted myself so lucky, but I still couldn't relax. Taking away wine had made my overactive mind wind itself up, and try as I might, I just struggled to stay calm. The littlest things brought me to tears, I felt like everyone was watching me, seeing me for the failure I was. But I had no choice to but to keep going, it was more than just me now, I had to do it for him.

My hips were causing me a lot of pain too, and I was diagnosed very early on with pelvic girdle pain. It caused no trouble to the baby, but made getting around hard for me, particularly up and down the stairs and getting in and out of the car. It was recommended I start pregnancy yoga and I was referred to the physiotherapist who was great and saw me weekly for a time. She would poke and prod me and it would provide relief for a short time, but then the pain would come back and it was agony. Sleeping became difficult and everything hurt. It wasn't discovered actually until I was in labour, but the baby was in the wrong position, and although not breech was facing the wrong way. His hands and feet were on the front of my tummy, which meant you could see every movement, which caused much amusement for the kids but was actually quite painful! He really seemed to like kicking just under the right hand side of my ribs and I couldn't find anywhere comfortable to be, due to his position. If it sounds like I am complaining, I'm not, it just bloody hurt. Pregnancy is not glamorous or comfortable at the best of times but putting a backwards baby into a broken body felt even worse.

To my surprise I was offered painkillers that 'might be addictive'. This came from people who had my notes in front of them. It wasn't a secret to them that I had been addicted to alcohol, even though I might not have chosen to bring it up. When I asked how it would affect the baby, they told me it wouldn't hurt him, but after he was born I might have to stay in hospital with him for a few days in case he suffered withdrawal symptoms. I couldn't believe I would be offered something that could affect my baby like that, and knowing how hard it was to stop drinking, there was no way I would ever intentionally put my child through it. It upset me to even think about it.

The physio suggested acupressure which seemed to provide more relief than anything else had done. It was different to anything I had ever experienced, but gave me time to relax while being pricked like a pin cushion. It was bizarre. But I kept going back because it seemed to be better than anything else had been. One week my therapist wasn't there, but left instructions for her colleague to treat me instead. I had my youngest son Barn with me as it was the holidays and I was grateful for it, because everything was different. Instead of lying down on my side, she had me sit in a chair, head forward onto a bed. I did as I was told, but it didn't feel comfortable. She then inserted the needles in my neck, back and legs as before but carried on into my lower leg and my foot. She told me not to lean back as the needles might hit the chair behind me and then left to catch up on my notes. I told myself not to, but almost straightaway I began to panic. I was terrified of moving, I didn't know how long the needles were, how far back the chair was and what damage I could cause myself. I tried to breathe through it, trying to use all the techniques I had to calm myself, but my breathing just got faster and faster, I was feeling sick and shaky. It was scary and I tried to cope because I didn't want to worry Barn but he must have noticed, because he began to ask me if I was all right. I told him I was probably just nervous but I could feel him watching me and soon he told me he was going to get the therapist. She came rushing back and removed the needles immediately, telling me to lie down and bringing me a glass of water. I was quite heavily pregnant at this point and felt stupid, like I was causing trouble, it's just like me to blame myself, but she told me she had used a different version of acupressure to the treatment the other therapist had been using. Her version was based more on the Chinese meridians and apparently could affect people like I had been. I wish she had warned me beforehand! I was so grateful that I wasn't on my own, I'm not sure what I would have done if my son hadn't been with me. It didn't do a lot for my faith in medical professionals and that was it for me. I don't know if my original therapist came back, because I didn't make any more appointments. It was a shame, because for something that had been beneficial, it was now just tainted with more worry. Feeling like that had been awful, and I didn't want to feel like it again.

Yoga was something I'd wanted to do for a long time, but I allowed myself to be put off by social media stereotypes. Looking on Instagram everyone was super lean, strong and flexible and I was a Mum, and not a particularly bendy one at that. My opportunity to start doing yoga regularly came unexpectedly really as I hadn't thought it would be a benefit for the pain I was having, but when the midwife suggested it, I thought it would be worth a not only for that, but to help manage my anxiety and just give me some time out. I quickly found a class nearby which I could attend in the evenings, once a week. I was so nervous going to the first class, and waited in the car outside to see the sort of people walking in, just to make sure I wasn't the only inflexible one. Once inside I realised that no one there was interested in what I was doing, everyone was actually just there for themselves, and once I'd come to terms with that, I actually began to relax and enjoy it.

One of the many benefits of joining a class during pregnancy is that there is no pressure to achieve, or push yourself, I didn't have to be thin and I didn't have to be flexible. It was just a time of quiet introspection and gave me a really lovely grounding into the basics of yoga. I learned breathing techniques in class which helped not only during my pregnancy, but also in labour, and after to settle my little one. In fact, I still use them at times now, they help when I get anxious as your breath is a great way of letting go.

I muddled through the rest of the pregnancy as best as I could until my midwife suggested I was induced as she was worried that leaving me go to full term would mean I wouldn't be able to deliver the baby naturally. The consultant agreed and at thirty six weeks I was admitted for induction. We had to wait three days on the ward before we could go up to the delivery suite, as they were bed-blocked, but they wouldn't discharge me, so we stayed, Lee sleeping in the chair next to me as it was almost an hour to drive to get home.

On 10th May 2017 at 11.56pm our littlest man joined us. It was amazing to finally meet this little person, and soppy as it sounds, it felt like the missing piece of our puzzle was there. The kids joked that he had always been on the way, he had just been 'lost in the post'. I think that is so sweet, and considering we were worried about the age gap, there has never been a little boy so loved.

CHAPTER 11
2018

I was happier than I had been in years, I had my amazing family, a wonderful husband, four amazing children and things were going well. Still though it was hard, things didn't come together straight away for me, and in fact, they are still coming together for me now. Taking away something that is such a large part of your life, even when you don't want it anymore is hard. You suddenly have more time, and my mind sort of woke up. I didn't even realise how much I had been numbing it, but gradually it got more and more chaotic, and without wine, that is something I am learning to deal with. It's tricky. And I'm not sure I have all the answers yet.

I felt cheated in many ways, I felt that I had done the hard bit, I'd kicked the habit I had been trying to for years. I'd faced up to it, struggled and overcome it, and yet, I felt worse. Everything was hard. I worried all the time. Panic attacks came out of nowhere, I cried a lot, and at nothing in particular. I was happy at home, but put me out of my comfort zone and I struggled, I felt like I was being watched everywhere I went, that people were looking at me and laughing. Before I stopped drinking my anxiety was bad, but I hadn't realised how drinking in the evening allowed me time not to think. Working through everything was hard. So hard. I felt like I was complaining about nothing in many ways too, because why should I feel like this, why should I complain when I had so much? On the outside it wouldn't look like I had a reason to worry or stress, but I just couldn't control the feelings I had in my head. It was so busy all the time.

In hindsight I think that it was almost easy to stop drinking when I was pregnant. I had done it three times before, and I knew I was putting someone else first. There was no way I would have done anything willingly to hurt the baby and that meant not drinking or even taking paracetamol when I had a headache. I was so worried that there would be something wrong with him, maybe caused by my years of drinking, so I did everything I could in my power to keep him safe. Of course though, once he was born, I was back to doing it for myself. Having nine months of sobriety under my belt was great, it was the longest I had ever done, but it also felt like I was back at square one. I didn't want to slip up and end up back at the start, but I no longer had the reason I was pregnant as an excuse or safety net to stop me drinking. I had to want to stay sober enough by myself, and although we now had a newborn, I had my body back and I wasn't breastfeeding so there was no reason why I couldn't drink, I just didn't want to anymore. Deciding I didn't want to didn't actually make it any easier really, it just strengthened my resolve, it was still hard, I still felt confused and a bit lost, but I just kept doing what I was doing and hoped I would get to a point that it would get easier. People said it did, so I held on to that, it just seemed to take a really long time for anything to change!

I carried on with yoga, trying to use it to help get my body back into shape but also trying to do everything I could to get my mind back. I longed for a bit of stillness. I signed up to app and meditated every day, and tried mindfulness. It all helped a little, but nothing really hit the nail on the head. They say that no one will love you until you love yourself. I don't think 'they' are always right about that. I had a family who loved me, a husband who stood by me through thick and thin, and was more supportive than I could ever have asked, and yet, I couldn't understand why they loved me. I was so ashamed of myself, I felt like I'd let myself down, my family down, I felt so down it was untrue. And my mind just circled. If someone said something to me, I'd go over and over it, wondering what and why, and trying to make sense of it. If we had an argument, I immediately felt ridiculous, like I was such an idiot, such a let down. The more I tried to get on top of it, the worse I felt.

I read a lot of books, mostly about mental health and anxiety, but really I'd pick up anything I thought might help me. I'd even read a few about activities and exercise helping mental health but I'd never been sporty. I'd never enjoyed exercise of any sort when I was younger. I would do anything I could to get out of PE at school, even if it meant writing lines in the sports hall which was often their way to keep those busy who weren't participating. PE really just seemed like another excuse for a popularity contest. I wasn't that popular at school, in fact I hated it. It got easier as the years went by, but I never felt a part of it, I never had a solid group of friends that I could rely on. PE meant watching as that was reinforced, I would be one of the last to be picked for team games, I didn't seem to know the rules, I wasn't fast enough to be one of the fit ones or slow enough to be one of the cool for not trying kids. I never had enough patience to stick at things, and if I decided I wanted to try a sport, I quickly grew tired when I didn't see a huge improvement in myself or my skill. The only exception to this was horses. I'd had horses for most of my teenage years, my Mum and Dad having a smallholding with sheep and chickens, and me having a horse, normally one at a time, which I would sell when outgrown before buying another, bigger one. Horses were my escape as I grew up. I didn't need friends when I had them. I didn't need anyone. I could go out and ride for hours, and explore the Cornish countryside. I was lucky to have such freedom, and I certainly made use of it. Unfortunately my last horse, a beautiful mare called Connie got colic and had to be put to sleep when I was 17. It broke my heart and I haven't had another horse since.

So, not a sporty person, and yet I was really getting into yoga. After my pre-natal yoga, I'd got into post-natal yoga too, and enjoyed taking Stanley along with me from the time he was five weeks old. It was a lovely time for us, but it wasn't enough. Gaining in confidence not only in my yoga ability, but in my body itself, I began to practice on my own as well, finding a class I could go to with Katie in the evening and began to try to push myself in ways I had never done before in my life. To start with I still worried about everything, even in the gentle classes I was in, I thought I wouldn't be able to complete the class, or I'd fall or embarrass myself. I was always concerned that if I did too much in the day, I wouldn't have enough left to do the class, I didn't have any faith in myself or my body. Around the same time, I read a book about a lady who found running really helped her mental health and something in me wondered if I could do that too. But of course like I said, I'd never run before, nor had I wanted to, so I wasn't sure what I was getting myself into. On a whim, I downloaded an app I heard about called C25k. Endorsed by the NHS it was supposedly a plan to get anyone from couch to running 5k, which is 3.1 miles, so I thought I'd give it a go. Before I never would have even gone outside in leggings, but yoga had helped with that. I didn't feel confident in myself so to speak, but I did feel a confidence growing in my body that I hadn't ever done before. It was stronger than I thought and I was able to do things I could never do before. I'd learned some pretty tricky yoga poses, and was so proud of myself the first time I managed to pull off a headstand, it was something I couldn't do as a child, and here I was in my thirties able to do it. It was quite strange, but in a good way.

The first day I decided to 'run' I plugged in my earphones and off I went. I was feeling quite positive, and then of course, the wind was knocked out of my sails. Maybe it was the strength I was gaining through yoga, but I must have had a bit of a distorted view of my fitness. The first session was broken down into a one minute run with a one and a half minute walk, repeated six times. It was hard, harder than I imagined. Running for a minute doesn't seem like a lot, until you try to do it for the first time. Then that minute is the longest amount of time in the world. It was painful, but I did it and I went home feeling proud. I carried on with the programme, trying to build up my strength, and as recommended, I booked a 5k race for near the end as something to aim for. I chose a race to raise money for a new air-ambulance for Cornwall, hoping that the fundraising would help me stick at it, as I've said before, I didn't previously have a lot of staying power when it came to sports and fitness, and was worried I would lose interest or find it too difficult and just give up. 5k isn't a huge distance for those who have been running for a while, but for me as a non-runner, it was a daunting task. I wasn't sure that I would be able to do it, or if I could, whether I would be fast enough. I imagined people laughing at me from the sidelines as I staggered past. Although it caused me stress, it also gave me enough incentive to keep going, which I suppose was the point. I did find I pushed myself too much at the beginning, running too many days in a row without having a break and I ended up injuring my knee, apparently a common thing among new runners, which ended up with me having to take an unscheduled break to rest and repair. I was really concerned that my progress would suffer, but two weeks or so later I was back out and trying again. I was more careful this time and took things a little more slowly.

The more I ran the better I got. I'd never followed a schedule like the C25k plan before, and I did it as closely as I could. Before, I had lost interest in activities because I didn't show improvement, but with this plan I could see it easily. At the start I struggled with one minute runs and then after a few weeks I found I could run for five minutes without stopping. It gave me something to focus on, and it got me out of the house. I found a field near our home and spent evenings running laps of it, sometimes dragging Barn who was thirteen then along with me. I'd signed him up for the race too, and was worried he wasn't taking it seriously enough. He didn't train as much as me, and when he did come out he was nagging me to run faster or further. He didn't realise how well my plan was working for me. It was hard as well for me to see him take to it so naturally, to not try as hard as I was or take it so seriously but just be able to do it with ease. Much as it frustrated me though, it was lovely to see him enjoying something.

Barn was different to our elder two children Joe and Katie. He had struggled in school for some years, unable to keep quiet in class, always a little bit eccentric, clever but hard to keep busy and on track. At the time it was just one more stress I didn't need. He was unhappy at school but always seemed to be getting into trouble. He wouldn't read, not that he couldn't, he just didn't want to and try as they might to encourage him, all the strategies they put in place just seemed to isolate him further from his classmates. He would have to be taken out individually to a staff room to read, and there was talk of putting partitions around his desk to stop him getting distracted. He was only five or six then. In the end we resorted to moving him from his first primary school to another one that was much smaller after his behaviour got worse and the school he was in failed to deal with him in a positive way. Here he had begun to settle, finally able to be free of the scape goat persona that had been created for him and find out who he was. He spent a lot of time outdoors there, but like me, wasn't interested in any real physical sports. To be honest, he'd rather be in the forest, and loved building bird hides and looking after the chickens. Seeing him begin to participate in running was brilliant, although he failed to see his natural ability for a very long time. Skipping on a bit, I can tell you now that his hard work paid off, and his confidence improved immensely with the volunteering work he did at our local parkrun as part of his Duke of Edinburgh Award. In the autumn of 2019, he was chosen to represent his school as part of the cross country team. He wasn't keen, but under encouragement joined a local running club and began to train three times a week with them, from there he flew. I was so proud when he qualified not only for the Cornwall Schools Team competing regionally and then nationally but also then as part of The Cornwall Cross Country team. In 2020 he travelled to Yeovil, Bournemouth, Loughborough and Liverpool with his team on their coach, and his confidence in himself has grown and grown. It makes me so proud to see something that started as a whim for me, turn into what could be a future career for him. We've nicknamed him 'Cornwall Legs', down to the speed he has and his natural ability to run.

Back to 2018. We'd never taken the kids abroad before, well at least on a plane. When Joe and Katie were small we drove to Spain, and when we had Barney too, we drove down to the South of France a few times. We didn't like the idea of inflicting three small kids on a plane full of people, and having the car gave us the freedom to explore with our tent, moving about the country as we chose, rather than being confined to one place or another. We'd always wanted to go somewhere on a plane, but the passports alone for a family of our size cost a small fortune, so we always put it off. When I was drinking it made me nervous as well, not that I would admit it to anyone else, but I didn't like not knowing where my next drink would come from, and the unpredictability made it difficult for me. As the kids got older, we wondered if we had missed our window, and if they'd even still want to all come away with us.

During the second year of being open we enforced a one week closure in the summer at our company. It's the only time besides Christmas that we get time off together, although the staff obviously get other holiday. Lee worries when he isn't there, so during this week, we know nothing is happening without him and he actually has no choice but to relax, although he seems to be on a mission to find other things to occupy him. We toyed with the idea of staying open and the staff running things, but then Lee's phone rings so much with questions that he may as well be in the office. In the first year we hadn't closed as such. We didn't have any staff then, and it was just the family we thought we'd divert the office phone to my mobile and answer any calls from there. It was a bit like a Carry-On movie. At one point we were in a boat we had rented with the kids, sailing up an estuary from Falmouth to Truro, when the phone rang and I had to put my work head on, and talk to someone about an exhibition stand they wanted, all while pretending I was in the office and hushing the children! A similar thing happened when we were in the park, but that was easier. Lee and I walked away a little, letting the kids play while we dealt with it. Looking back it makes me smile now, but we did cause ourselves some stress, trying to make things work!

We began to realise that time was slipping away by putting things off and so Lee and I popped to the travel agent. Even last minute holidays are expensive for a family of six, but we managed to get one to Corfu leaving the next day. It was the start of our summer break, so we had a whole week without work to worry about. Going home to tell the kids and seeing the shock on their faces was great. They were used to us doing things last minute, but not normally jumping on a plane! It was a good test for me and my anxiety as there wasn't too much time to get too worked up. For me this is always a bonus, because I over worry all the time anyway, so it was a relief to go without having too much time to build it up. We were flying from Bristol so left in the early evening giving us plenty of time to get there. We had a few car troubles at the time, and were hoping our dodgy VW Transporter would get us there. It had spent most of the year in and out of the garage and had had most of the engine rebuilt, but it was still temperamental. I wasn't sure how I'd be either, and had aromatherapy oils in my pockets to help me out, which was fine until I forgot to get them out of my pocket and security found them! I lost my sunglasses too, because I forgot to take them out of the buggy when it went through the x-ray machine, but luckily they were soon found. Being busy helps, so although I am scatty, having to find things I've lost, or organise the kids stops me from panicking. I didn't find the airport too bad at all, until we made our way through to the departure lounge. When I am still, or confined I get really twitchy and here we were just waiting without anything to occupy my mind. The moment we sat down I started to worry, my heart raced and I had a bit of a meltdown, ending up in floods of tears. I hate how out of control I feel in situations like that, it's so frustrating, it's not even like it's because of something logical, like perhaps being afraid to fly, because I'm not. Soon the doors were open and we could get onto the bus to the plane. After that I was okay, and seeing the enjoyment on the kids faces made it so worth it. The flight itself wasn't hard for me, which was surprising, as I had been worried that I would feel trapped, and obviously not be able to do anything about it. Landing in Corfu, we realised that Stanley's pram had come apart in the hold of the plane, and we were now missing parts to fit it together. That was frustrating, but luckily, the advantage of having a big family is that there were enough of us to hold Stanley and the bags and make our way through to the bus to our hotel. We boarded our coach to the hotel and Joe's face was a picture as we wound our way through tiny streets with vehicles coming in every direction towards us, he hadn't long been driving, so it was certainly an experience for him!

Our hotel was right on the beach, with three swimming pools in its grounds. It was an amazing place to relax and enjoy being together. We didn't do much other than swim and relax, but we did it together. We did find some wonderful places to eat, and I found myself enjoying food more than I ever had before, experimenting with different dishes and for the first time enjoying the freedom I had from wine. One evening while sat outside after dinner, I did struggle a little with everyone else drinking in the hotel grounds. Through dinner it didn't bother me, and I often had a soft drink in a wine glass the same as the rest of the family. Somehow, sitting outside in a social environment with music playing was different and it caught me off guard. It made me want a glass of wine very badly. Again, Lee was supportive. He didn't make decisions for me, and was supportive of me if I did want to drink. To be honest, I was right on the edge of having a glass. I didn't understand why they could and I couldn't. It was hard and I got quite upset, but then I reminded myself that I could drink, I just chose not to. Although I kidded myself that it would only be one, that I deserved it and would enjoy it, I knew that one glass still wouldn't be enough for me, and it would awaken the desire that I had been fighting against for so long. I had to remind myself who had the control, who made the choice and ultimately who benefitted from the fact I no longer drank. I knew too, that other than that wobble, I was having a far better holiday than I would have done if I drank, and also, that I was coping better with the time away. Things like being somewhere new, not knowing where I was going, losing the bits of the buggy, all these things I managed on my own. Before I would have been drinking to get through, and while I would have enjoyed myself, I wouldn't have really been there and I wouldn't have remembered things with such clarity.

One day as we were walking down the beach the kids saw a boat go out, taking people out parasailing. Katie and Joe wanted to go so we went to enquire about how much it was. Lee had been years ago on a previous holiday, but I hadn't been before, so he encouraged me to go and said he was happy to stay with Stanley. It was optional to go up in pairs so Barn decided to go with Katie leaving me to go with Joe. I needed a lot of convincing, I was so nervous! It was like nothing I had ever done before. We were taken out in a speedboat to an island pontoon where they put on our harnesses. Katie and Barn went first and once they were in the air it was time for me and Joe to go. They harnessed us up and Joe set his Go-Pro up, having brought it with us at the last minute. We hadn't planned on anything like this, so it was just lucky we had it with us. We were told that we had to put our left foot forward, and run when the boat started to go. When we reached the edge of the pontoon we were just to let go, not to jump. It was scary, I was so nervous I'd get it wrong, but then we were off and before I'd had time to think we were up in the air, looking back across the bay at our hotel and the beach and seeing Katie and Barn up in the sky too. It was over all too quickly, with us being dropped into the sea, to swim back to the boat, but it was an experience I'll never forget and I wouldn't have done it if I'd still been drinking. In fact, I don't think I would have even made it onto the plane!

Back home I continued to run. It took time, but a landmark for me was one run on the treadmill when I looked down and thought, "It's okay, only eight minutes to go." As soon as I had thought it, I was shocked, since when had I thought eight minutes was a short time to run? The little achievements like that added up and gave me confidence, and Barn and I ran that first race together, well Barn left me behind, but we were there together, raising a lot of money for the charity. After that I gradually began to up my distance, trying to test myself. I didn't think I would ever want to run long distances, to be honest, before I started running I couldn't see the point, or the draw other people saw in it, and yet here I was looking for races to sign up for. The biggest thing for me was finding races that we could do together, due to Barn's age of 13 he wasn't allowed to do many due to the distance, and at the time I wasn't keen to do them on my own. It was around this time that my daughter Katie began to run too, and it became much more of a family event. We'd find races we could do together and make a nice trip of it, even if it was just a parkrun. Afterwards we would stop for a cup of tea in the cafe. These seem like simple things, but they weren't for me. In the last years of my drinking I would never have eaten out, I would have been too anxious, and the same went for after I gave up. Finding time like this, and having an excuse to get out made it easier to reclaim a bit more of the life I had lost.

Parkrun drew me out of myself a little more too. When I was younger I used to enjoy volunteering for things, but there was always a reason for it. Perhaps I saw it as a way into something or a way up the career ladder, I'm not sure, but I seldom did things without a benefit. When I started running I found out about parkrun. For those of you who don't know, parkrun is a free initiative across the world where you turn up and run, walk or jog 5k. They are organised at the same time across the world every Saturday morning. All you need is a barcode which is free, and you can have your time recorded each week. Most people have one pretty close by, even if they don't know about it. I was surprised to realise that there were two parkruns close to my home, and more that were in easy travelling distance, but even more shocked to realise that they were all run every week by volunteers. I couldn't imagine what these people got out of it, surely they had better things to do than volunteer every week? Surely they would all prefer to be out there running themselves than watch others run? After a lot of persuasion I started going to parkrun as a means to get myself out more and build my running up. It was a great way of improving but I always felt a little bit lacking on the community side, and not that I expected instant friends, but I did struggle to break the ice at parkrun, beyond saying hello to familiar faces.

Barn had started his Duke of Edinburgh Award at the start of the school year, and needed to volunteer somewhere. Parkrun was a great option for him as it was something he cared about and they actively recruited new volunteers. To start with I still ran each week while he took on different roles. Then one week I saw the roster looking empty and before I thought too much about it, I put my name down. I don't know what I was expecting, and certainly nothing hit me straightaway, but after a few weeks, I realised that I no longer felt like an outsider. Parkrun suddenly started to feel a little bit like it was mine too. It no longer mattered that I didn't know anyone, it didn't matter that I wasn't the fastest. Instead, I was part of the community, I was out there, helping to make an event happen, come rain or shine. I don't volunteer every week, but I do so quite often and have quite enjoyed taking on new roles. I was there to help when someone had a nasty fall, and I've been the tailwalker at the end, to encourage those who struggled. I've also stopped behind afterwards to sort out several hundred finishing tokens into the right order, ready to be used the following week. My hard work has started to pay off and I began to notice I don't analyse all my conversations with 'real' people quite so much. Instead I walk away feeling quite chuffed with myself that I've managed to have a chat with someone. It's such a small thing to many, but to me, it gives me a bit of a warm glow inside, however soppy that sounds!

When the clocks changed and the nights drew in earlier, I struggled to get out. I know a lot of people run in the dark but I wasn't keen. Especially on my own. At the time, it was just one step too far. So we looked out for a used treadmill and I also got a second hand buggy to run with. It was heavier than some of the expensive models, but I wasn't sure how much I'd use it and it meant I could run with Stanley. That was a new experience, but great to have another excuse to get out.

Over the winter I ran my first 10k, a distance I never thought I'd run, and yet here I was doing it. Barn was too young to race with me, and Katie didn't want to run that far, so I made myself go by myself. It was scary, but I was so proud of myself for doing it. I had joined a local running club, but didn't feel like I felt in and struggled mixing with groups of people who knew each other. I found it difficult as so many of them joked about drinking and liked to pop to the pub after a run, while not drinking was still new to me. I wanted to avoid anything alcohol related, and anything that would make me stand out from the crowd. I knew other people still liked to drink, and I didn't actually mind them doing it, I was just oversensitive about how I looked and how I felt about it. I felt safer at home and so my time running with that club didn't last very long. Shortly after I found the Lonely Goats, mad as it sounds it's an online running club for people who don't want to run with others or can't. There are people like me, who aren't great with groups, there are shift workers and parents without childcare, you name it, there's someone in there to represent it. We don't run together, but that doesn't mean the support isn't there. If a 'goat' wants to talk, there is always someone to listen. There are so many people in the group that there is always someone who knows what it is you're after, or understands your situation. After a time Barn and Katie joined too so we aren't such lonely goats after all! After races sometimes we'd see others to chat to, and say hello, or pause for a group photo which would be posted to the group on social media afterwards. It began to bring me out of myself, chatting to people, and getting to know people who were seeing the real me instead of the drunk me. Or the wanting to have a drink me. It was a relief, but I was still careful about who I told about my drinking problem, I was too nervous of being judged, and sadly I carried a lot of shame about it still. I was so afraid people wouldn't want to know me if they knew what I had been like and that they wouldn't understand. I hadn't even spoken to our kids about it.

Bearing in mind this was the first year in a long time that I hadn't drunk alcohol, I had replaced it with a wine with the alcohol removed. I know this is a bit of a controversial subject for many as some people think it is still a reliance on a substance, but for me it really helped me get over my addiction. I could still have my wine glass in the evening, but without the hangover or sore head, it was quite a nice in-between, although of course, it didn't really give me any of the relaxing feelings that wine did. I spent a lot of time googling the side-effects and found there really weren't any, and in fact, the one I had chosen was supposedly full of anti-oxidants, but without the side-effects of wine, so I really couldn't see any harm in it. Of course, overtime, I began to rely on it in the same way that I had wine, I told myself it was different, that it was okay because it wasn't addictive and it wasn't damaging to my health, but that didn't stop my mind worrying and whirring about it. I didn't realise quite how reliant I had got to be honest, until the familiar feelings of having to plan how many bottles I had in the fridge came back.

Towards the end of the year, I went shopping with Joe and Stanley. We'd only popped in to get a few things from the local supermarket, unfortunately having so many shops locally meant I often did that, rather than organise myself and buy a proper weekly shop. Stanley was only about four or five months old and in the trolley, and Joe and I were chatting as we walked around. Once we finished we went to the self service conveyor, and I started to scan the items. It was getting late, and Stanley started to cry, I turned to soothe him, not even thinking anything of the fact Joe carried on scanning where I had left off. In fact it wasn't until a very abrupt cashier came over to me and literally demanded ID that I realised he had scanned the bottles of non-alcoholic wine as well as my cereal, toilet rolls and other household items. I was surprised, but handed it over, to which she asked to see Joe's, claiming that he had in her words 'handled' the wine. I laughed and replied that of course he had, I was comforting the baby, but as he was sixteen at the time he didn't have any ID. I am not kidding you she was so rude. I pointed out that it was alcohol free wine, that it was for me, I was paying, and that it was obvious from the shopping that it was my shopping for a family, not a trolley full of party items for a load of teenagers, but she ignored me. She told me she would check with her supervisor, but then returned saying I couldn't have it because Joe was too young. I was astounded, not really because she had taken it, but because of her attitude. I don't deal well with confrontations of any kind and by this point I was shaking. I almost wanted to leave the rest of the shopping, but there were things in it I needed, so we paid and went to leave. As we were leaving though, we passed the customer service desk, and I decided that actually she had no right to speak to me the way she did, so I thought I would complain. It isn't something I do often, but she had been really out of order, to the point another cashier had stopped me on the way out and told me they would have let me have it, so it made me feel that it couldn't have just been me being over-sensitive. I could see Joe was getting worried, I was so worked up by now that I was shaking and right on the edge of tears. I just wanted to be heard, and understood, and I was so frustrated that I hadn't been. I was explaining everything to the lady at the counter when the supervisor the cashier had checked with came up. The cashier herself must have seen me, because she also appeared, and when questioned told the other staff that Stanley hadn't been crying at all. She implied that her choices were totally reasonable and that she was in the right. That did nothing for my anger! There is nothing I hate more than being misunderstood, but being called a liar was ridiculous! The manager apologised immediately, telling me she hadn't been made aware that it was alcohol free wine and that if she had known it would not have been a problem, they offered to retrieve the bottles, and sell them to me anyway, but I was done. Somewhere in the back of my mind I was thinking that this wasn't a normal reaction to have to not being allowed something. I certainly wanted it, but I wouldn't have got so upset if it was chocolate, or milk. I couldn't go elsewhere either, and that made it worse, but also made me justify it to myself which didn't help. So I just told them to stick it and walked out with the shopping I had paid for. I was so angry I refused to go into that store, or any of their branches for over a year and a half. My husband and kids also boycotted them with me, even though it meant we had to do our shopping much further away which was a pain in the neck. I know the staff probably didn't even notice my disappearance, but it made me feel like I was doing something. Even though it was a bit nuts.

CHAPTER 12
2019

I didn't really talk about my 'problem'. I knew for certain I had a drinking problem by now, there was no questioning that, but I still wasn't comfortable talking about it. I didn't know what people would think, and I didn't like the images that certain words conjure up. By using a word to describe a condition, we create a label which begins to define us as a person. A label can limit us, and make us think that is all we are. I struggled with the word 'alcoholic'. It didn't sit well with me at all. I worked, I had happy kids and a clean house, how could I possibly be defined as an alcoholic? When I think of the word it conjures images in my mind that I would rather not be associated with and yet I could be. Although I am different in many ways, I am also the same. I preferred the term addict, although to be an alcohol addict is much the same as an alcoholic, it felt like the label wasn't just on me, it was also on the condition. It wasn't just my failure, it was also the substance's fault. Before, if tried to define myself I almost whispered the word 'alcoholic', I was afraid it could make everyone see there was something wrong with me. More recently

I'm trying to come to terms with it, thinking that if I am okay with it, it takes the power away from the word. Gradually it has begun to bother me less and the more I use the term, the less power it seems to have. I found the same with the term tea-total. Now there is nothing wrong with it at all, especially when I enjoy tea as much as I do, but I felt it just a little limiting. I don't want to be limited by something, I had plenty of that when I worried where my next glass of wine was coming from. Personally I quite like the term alcohol free. Finally, that's how I feel now, free of it, like I've shaken it off and it isn't holding me back anymore. That doesn't mean I don't have little moments of wine glass envy, but that is all it is now, and as soon as I remind myself, I'm okay with it again. I feel term alcohol free implies it's my choice to be without the burden of alcohol, which of course it is. It makes me feel like I've cast something off, rather than have something weigh me down. Isn't it funny the power these small words have? I never thought the terminology of something would bother me so much, but I know we are all different, even down to the perceptions we create by using a simple word.

On top of everything else, I wasn't sure what to do regarding the kids. I loved them so much, and I was so afraid they'd be disappointed in me for my drinking, and yet, I hated keeping secrets from them. I was also a bit afraid that there might be some hereditary gene causing a predisposition to drinking in my family and that I might be doing them a disservice by not making them aware of the possibility. It was clear that other relatives of theirs also drank a bit, and while that isn't my problem or battle, I just wanted the kids to be aware, so they didn't end up falling into the same trap as I did.

No one could have told me to stop before I was ready to do it myself. It was hard enough to face then when I was ready, and if anyone had tried to make me do it sooner it would have been impossible. In my mind, there was never a good time to bring it up, so I just didn't. It was hard to talk to Lee at that time though, because any time I found something hard or difficult, I had to be away from the kids or speak in code to tell him what I was thinking. It seemed contradictory because on the whole I am really open with the kids and maintain the fact that if they are sensible enough to ask me about something, then I will explain it to them. One day I was driving Barn home, I can't even remember where from and he brought it up. He stumbled over his words and I could see he found it hard. He didn't want to upset me, but clearly wanted to know. I wasn't sure what to say, he had caught me off guard, but I'd done it for every other subject the kids had spoken to me about, and couldn't see why this should be different so I tried to explain. I asked him not to talk to his brother and sister about it, that it was between us until I spoke to them, but explained they hadn't asked and until then I just found it difficult. I told him everything. It felt like a weight had been lifted off my shoulders. He was so mature and understanding, and suddenly he seemed to be more patient with me than he had before.

Not long after that Katie and I were talking. It's weird, it was also in the car. That must be my place for serious conversations. We were really into the series Grey's Anatomy, and one of the doctors in the show had been struggling with an addiction. We'd been joking about something, and Katie had commented something like, at least I wasn't as bad as Amy from the show. Taking the opportunity, I told her I was. She looked at me, and sort of repeated what she meant, to which I told her again, I was. It was difficult, but again, once the can of worms had been opened, everything began to come out. It wasn't the sort of conversation I had hoped to have with my daughter, but again, it seemed to bring a whole other level of understanding to our relationship, and I would say, it brought us even closer.

The only one I hadn't spoken to was Joe. He's quite a quiet lad, sensitive, but he keeps it on the inside. I waited and waited for an opportunity to speak to him, but none arose and I didn't like the fact that I had spoken to his brother and sister and not him. It made me feel like I was keeping him in the dark somehow. Eventually I decided to try to broach the subject with him. I waited until we were alone, and carefully tried to talk to him. He was very dismissive, and kind of said the bare minimum to end the conversation as soon as he could. It was fine and he is fine about it, but what it did do was bring home to me how much more he must remember than the others, being the oldest, and that makes me feel very sad. I wish he didn't remember that. I wish I could protect him from it, but I can't change anything I did, just what I do from now on, and I know we are okay.

Sometimes now, I'll make jokes around the kids about my drinking, nothing too serious, just enough for them to know that I am okay with it. I want to have the most open relationship I can with them, and I want them to know that they can talk to me about anything. It's lovely that the kids know I am not so sensitive about it now too, and although they joke, they aren't insensitive, they are just perhaps more aware that people might suffer from an addiction or a mental health issue and still appear relatively 'normal' to the outside world.

Katie is an art student at college, and a few months ago was asked to bring a can in for a secret project for one class. It turned out she was making a pin hole camera which was really cool and she developed some fantastic photos from it, but beforehand she didn't know what the can was for. When she came home she was almost offended on my behalf because her tutor had apparently asked the class to bring in a large can, and made a joke about the students parents all having plenty of beer cans around at home. Katie told me how disappointed she was in her teacher because of the jokes. It's kind of the kids to think, but I don't want them to be overanxious on my behalf either. I don't want them to think that other people's actions and their choice to drink will affect me now, as I have been working hard not to let it. I think my reaction to Katie on this occasion while laughing was to say something like, "Tell your teacher we don't have cans of beer in the house because your mother is a raging alcoholic!" She wouldn't say anything like that to anyone, but it's nice to joke and made her laugh, Joe though caught my eye and looked at me as if I was nuts. He isn't quite so comfortable joking about it as his brother and sister are. It's a painful reminder that he remembers more than he lets on. I often think my temper wasn't the best, like I said, I was never violent or anything like that with them, but I know my attention wandered more than it should have and I was shorter of patience than I should have been. Especially in the evenings. Remembering that makes me sad, even though I know I can't change it and that I am doing the best I can now.

Speaking about it has given me a lot more freedom which feels really good. Before, I always felt like I was stepping on eggshells, I didn't want to admit to my problem but with it in the shadows I also couldn't really comment on a lot of things. We'd be watching TV and there might be a portrayal of an addict that was done really well, or really badly, (they do get blamed for everything) and I felt like I couldn't comment. Now I have the freedom to say what I think about it, and my family knows I am talking from experience. I do find TV shows difficult. They often make addicts out to be awful people who let everyone down and that isn't always true. Sometimes they are doing the best they can. Not so long ago, my middle son Barn told me that he found me inspirational. He quickly followed that comment by adding, "Wow, that sounded cheesy!" But when I pushed him to see what he meant he explained, that it showed him he could overcome something difficult, like I had. I hope none of my kids ever go through something like I did, but if my hard-times have shown my kids that they can overcome literally anything if they put their minds to it, then at least there is a point to it. At the very least, I hope they can see that I would understand and that would make it easier for them to talk to me.

Recently I remembered something that happened years ago. It was only a little something, but one of those things that sticks in your mind, and I just remember thinking at the time that my sister-in-law was so confident to act in the way she did. I wished I could be like that, but I couldn't. I felt like my self-doubt was really noticeable to others, even though it wasn't. As I got older I always compared myself to other people, I looked at everyone with curiosity, not judgment, but I tried to pick apart how and why people behaved in the ways they did. I wondered what people saw when they did the same to me, and I often thought they'd find me lacking. I hated feeling like that, but it just seemed obvious. Everyone else was strong and confident and I wasn't.

It's funny though, when I look back now on those times, I realise they didn't see me in the same way as I felt about myself.

I used to have a lot of friends and even more acquaintances. I think I saw my friends list as a badge of success. If I knew all these people, then they must like me, I must be popular. I think ultimately, since school I'd always struggled with how I felt about myself, and how I felt other people perceived me. I never quite felt good enough, I don't know why, but there was always a little voice of doubt nagging me, reminding me that other people were judging me, and generally looking down at me. I probably should have been able to shake the feelings off, and left it behind when I was no longer a teenager, but I didn't. Instead I just covered it up and buried it. On the outside I projected a look of self-confidence, because worse than feeling bad about myself would have been other people knowing about it. So following the "Fake it till you make it," school of thought, I just kept on trying cover up how I felt.

Wine acted as a huge buffer for me, between myself and my feelings. Although events themselves might have been hard, later when I got to overthinking and winding myself up, wine numbed it. It made it easier, but in the long run so much harder. Alcohol not only fuelled my anxiety, but it also prevented me from realising how bad it was. Over the last few years I shut myself off from everyone I knew. It was hard to go out and face everyone, not only was I more anxious than I had ever been before, but I was also filled with a huge amount of self-loathing for the amount I was drinking as a coping mechanism. I couldn't open up to anyone about how I felt, I was terrified that they would judge me and think the worst of me. Instead I avoided everyone. After I stopped drinking I had no reason to reconnect with anyone. I really felt any of my old friends wouldn't understand how much I'd changed, and that they didn't really know the real me anyway.

My kids joked with me that I have no friends, and to a certain extent that is true, I found it easier just to stay in my little bubble. Even making small talk became difficult, I'd often circle over conversations I'd had in passing, wondering why I'd said something and thinking how stupid I must have seemed. I hadn't expected my confidence to take such a knock, but then I guess, I should have been prepared, this new stripped back me had nowhere to hide.

Running got me outdoors, it helped my anxiety, it gave me a focus. Something I had never done before, and wasn't good at, suddenly became something I enjoyed and was getting better at, but people, well, I still avoided them where I could.

I've always been a bit suspicious of situations, people, you name it, I overthink it. I don't mean be the way I am necessarily, but I do have a habit of jumping to the worst conclusion at times. I even know that a lot of the time I'm wrong, but the problem is, sometimes I am right, and that reinforces my thinking. I think for me that one of the benefits of no longer drinking is that I see things more clearly now, but also with that tinge of suspicion. I'm never quite sure how to take people.

While I count myself lucky to have my family around me, isolating myself seemed the safest option for me, rightly or wrongly, I couldn't focus on lots of other people back then, I just had to think about myself and my family or I wouldn't have got through it. Most people understood, and if they didn't to be honest, there isn't a lot I could do about it, but some people, just a select few, that I had counted as friends didn't act like friends, instead they were selfish and used my vulnerability at that time to their advantage. Those are not the sort of people I want in my life, and I'm glad they are gone. The problem is, removing negative people, deleting or blocking friends from your list, etc, only removes those people from your life. There are always other people out there in the wings waiting, and I find it tricky to judge their motives. I know logically that not everyone is out to get me, but I often wonder why someone would talk to me out of the blue and what they hope to get out of it. I sound awfully cynical don't I? But I second guess everything, from how someone looks at me, to how I talk to them and the impression I give them.

One morning after parkrun I was deliberating over cake in the queue at the cafe when the man behind me spoke to me. We were just passing the time of day, talking about cake and I didn't think anything of it until he asked if he could join me to drink his coffee. I was shocked, not that there is anything wrong with it. Parkrun promotes community and chatting after a run, so why shouldn't someone want to sit with me, it just threw me as I wasn't expecting it. I said that it was fine, and pointed him in the direction of the table where my son was sitting, and by the time I had got there they were both chatting. We talked about running and a few other things, but when I was asked questions, I found myself worrying about what he wanted to know, and why he wanted to know it. I told you I was suspicious! Many other people were sitting in groups also chatting over their drinks, and it was perfectly normal, I do think, at least in this instance it is my problem and not his, but it is annoying to feel on guard all the time. After the man left I questioned whether the situation had been okay with my son. He gets how I worry, and is quite good at reassuring me, or telling me to stop being a fool depending on the situation. But despite his reassurances, I just wonder then if it's because he is younger that he doesn't realise how some adults can have ulterior motives.

It's taken me a long time to start to trust people, and their motives again and even those that know me will know I am not the most sociable person even now. It isn't that I don't want to be, I just worry. I am guarded, I know that, and I don't let many people in, it takes time for me to let my walls down a little and make friends. I am getting better at it, though slowly. I've even been known to have coffee after parkrun with people I do know. It's just when someone is forward, and it is unexpected, it throws me!

In the summer we went on holiday to Spain. Having had such a lovely holiday the year before we wanted to do something similar again. We popped to the travel agent and managed to book another last minute deal just over a week away. It gave us long enough to prepare, but still wasn't too far away for us. We caught an early morning flight from Manchester, I'd agreed to it having managed to save us quite a bit of money, but hadn't appreciated how much further it was on from Birmingham where we were originally going to fly from. The kids enjoyed walking through the shops there at 3am as that was something they'd never experienced before, and soon we were on our way. I can safely say I didn't miss drinking at all on the holiday, it was lovely.

Every evening we ate at a different restaurant and it was a great experience. Lee spent time looking on Trip-Advisor and we'd then put it to the vote to see where we should go. The atmosphere was lovely, and it was nice not only to be able to experiment with different foods, but to remember everything clearly. Doing this really helped me get over my issue with eating out, as I was pushing myself each and every night and I didn't want to let anyone down.

I'm not one for organised activities, and yet somehow me and the kids got roped into the 'pool party' fun at the hotel. It was hilarious and run by a very energetic Spanish man who led us in different dances while in the pool. I wouldn't have attempted to dance out of the water for fear that people could see me, and at home there is no way that Katie or Barn would ever join me for something like that, but with a little encouragement they did and they had fun. It was brilliant. At the end there was always a cool down to which we basically played games in the pool. On our last day we ended up in a huge circle with our arms around each other, letting every other person float as we pulled them along. It was fun, and I have a video Lee took without me realising to prove it. Even now if a familiar song comes on the radio Stanley shouts, "swimming pool" at the top of his voice! Who knew it would make such an impression on him?

I carried on with my yoga practice back at home and managed to find a class with a lovely teacher not far from where we lived. Katie enjoyed coming with me too, and I really enjoyed having something special for just the two of us. If you'd asked me a couple of years ago what a dynamic vinyasa flow class was I would have had no clue. Perceptions of yoga vary from person to person, with many people assuming that yoga is merely stretching. This class was not that. Instead it was a full body workout that made you sweat, while focusing on calming and centring your mind. Each week would have a new theme, and sometimes we would practice outside on the grass, overlooking the sea. It was a lovely place to practice and we were going every week and despite a couple of changes in times, it was great. One week the only people who turned up were me and Katie so we had a private session! Then of course things changed as seems inevitable when you come to look forward to something and I had a message to say that the venue we had been using was no longer available. It seemed a terrible shame as the teacher was truly talented and both Katie and I had really enjoyed the classes. Not long after, I found out a new venue had been found, which was fantastic, until I was told it was in in a pub. Maybe it's just me, but the idea of yoga in a pub just seems bizarre. It turned out it was a friend of a friend who offered the venue, but still, for me the idea of practicing in a pub is weird, and I just didn't think I would be comfortable relaxing in such a close vicinity to all that alcohol. It's not that I thought I would want to drink it, but being sober now, I don't particularly want to spend my free time in a pub, especially for something like yoga. Maybe I'm being over-sensitive?

Adding to it was the response I got from a post on my blog about it. I was so careful not to name the class or the location, let alone the teacher and no one that went to the class followed me. Not long after I posted my thoughts on yoga in a pub, and how it bothered me, I had several nasty messages from the teachers partner and best friend telling me that I should come, that it was fine and that I was being harsh to suggest it wasn't appropriate. While they were quick to criticise me, they didn't seem to understand that for an alcoholic, and I had told them that I was one, perhaps an evening in a pub wasn't quite how I wanted to spend my time. I've been told that they've since found space in a yoga studio but to be honest, after the response

I got from a post that wasn't aimed at or referencing them, I had no desire to go back. It shows the lack of understanding people can have for people that they don't understand and a lack of tolerance.

I was still running, still doing yoga and still hoping I could pull off this new calm, sober me. It was still harder than I thought it would be. I was still setting myself goals, and having completed the 5k race, and then the 10k race I had set for myself, I set my eyes on a bigger target, one I never thought I would do. I signed up for a Half Marathon. My iPhone apps had worked well for me so far, so I continued as I was doing and bought the next one in the set, called the 21k runner. A half marathon is 13.1 miles. That's quite a long way to walk, let alone run, but once I got it into my head I was set on it. I even had one fairly local to me, one that hadn't been on in a few years, and was now being organised again in Plymouth. They'd set up a series, including a 5k and a 10k, and I'd signed up to and run the 5k not long after the one for the Air Ambulance. Running the half seemed like a good plan and I had plenty of time to plan and train for it so there was nothing to worry about, except worrying is what I am good at. I am awful when it comes to races. I panic beforehand, I seldom think that I will be able to complete the distance, whatever that may be and feel like I will be last, with people laughing at me. It hasn't happened yet, but that doesn't stop me thinking it might. I panic on the drive to the race, I panic until I have found and visited the nearest toilet, sometimes I have to go even before I need to, because I know I will worry more if there is a queue later. I always worry I am going to drop my phone down into the portaloo and wonder how I will get it back and even if I will want to get it back.

I don't know where that worry in particular has come from as I have never (yet) dropped anything down a portaloo, but I am just scared I will. So as you can see I'm a bundle of nerves beforehand, it probably makes you wonder why I keep putting myself through it. I don't really know, in fact I thought once I got more used to running and races that I would get more used to it and the worrying would ease off. All I do know is that once I am running, that worry generally goes away. I've only once had a panic attack while running, that was scary! Normally I can kind of shut my mind off and let my body do the work once I get going and then it is just nice to enjoy the scenery. I'm always a little bit envious of runners that have friends to run with, as I think sometimes that distraction would help, but sometimes I think the chatter might wind me up more too. It's a difficult balance.

But anyway, here I was on the way to my first half marathon. The weekend previously I had run ten miles and then rested other than a couple of short runs during the week as my plan had detailed. I was ready. Except we were stuck in traffic at 7:30 on a Sunday morning on our way into Plymouth. Clearly everyone else in the local vicinity was also running or coming to support, and of course there were a lot of road closures because of the course being on closed roads. It did nothing to ease my worries, and in the end Lee told me to get out at the traffic lights sending Barn with me to walk to the start of the race, knowing I would want to look for the toilets while he and the other kids went to park the car. Walking helped a bit, and I was able to relax as we walked to Plymouth Hoe, seeing the start all set up, I even got to the toilets before the queue started. Later it was so much bigger, so I was glad I stopped when I had. I pinned my race number on and ate my banana and then Barn waited with me as we just watched the goings on. Before long Lee and the kids had managed to join us, and in no time at all I had to get to the start. It was packed, there was no space at all to move and all you could smell was muscle rub creams. It was like playing a game of sardines, as people tried to check their watches others would get elbowed, and yet more and more people came in too, all wanting to be close to their pacer depending on the time they hoped to get. I on the other hand had no idea what time I wanted to get; I had no idea whether I would even be able to finish having never run so far in my life. I just wanted to finish and told myself not to get carried away with the crowd, I didn't want to run too fast, too soon, and wear myself out. That was my only plan. I had jelly babies and a sports drink to keep me going, and other than that I was just going to keep putting one foot in front of another.

Soon the start was announced and we were off, although due to the amount of people we actually barely moved, it took over three minutes for me to cross the start line and be able to actually get going. Then we were running on the closed roads through the streets I knew so well, but had only driven before. There were people everywhere, there was so much to see that I stopped worrying and just ran. Miles passed and it wasn't until the mile five/six sort of point that it dawned on me how far I still had to go. There was one point there where we ran up one side of the dual carriageway for about a mile and then back down the other side, it was the most boring part and the sun beat down on us all both ways, first on one side of my face and then on the other. I wondered then if I would be able to keep going, but almost as soon as I had that thought I saw Barn waiting for me on a bridge, shouting and waving to keep me going. It was the boost

I needed, followed by a turn into an area I didn't know at all. That completely took my mind off everything, as we came out of the city and onto lanes before entering the beautiful grounds of a National Trust property. At that point I decided to have a bite of flapjack which caused the worst pain in my stomach I've ever had when running, I regretted it immediately, but of course had no choice but to keep going albeit slightly slower than I had been going. They say not to try new things on a race, especially one of this length. I really should have listened! A young runner who had been behind me, overtook me smiling and shouting, "You got this!" Again, the encouragement came just at the right moment, and we ran together for some time before becoming separated by the crowd. I wasn't sure where we were or how far we had left at this point, I didn't want to look at my watch in case it burst my bubble, but soon enough we began to come back into town and I realised I had less than three miles left. Less than a parkrun! I realised I could do it, so I kept on. The local firefighters were out and had hoses trained on us all as we ran past, man, that was cold, but refreshing, and made me glad I put my phone in a sandwich bag to keep it dry! Barn was waiting again for me to pass, giving me another boost of encouragement and even running with me for a short distance in his jeans to keep me going, another welcome distraction, and then we were back on familiar territory. Running on cobbles along the Barbican, I had never appreciated how hilly that was, and of course it was where most people were waiting to wave and cheer. I ran past Lee and the kids, pleased I was still running given the distance, and pleased I was still smiling given the hill that seemed to go on forever. Someone shouted my name, and I saw one of Barn's teachers cheering me on, followed by Lee's cousin, an official photographer for the day. It was all the distraction I needed to get me up the last bit of the hill and over the finish line. And then I stopped. I didn't know where to go so just followed everyone else, being handed my medal and t-shirt and cans of drink. By the time I had got out Lee and the kids were all waiting for me and suddenly everything began to spin. I've later learned this can happen when you stop running after such a distance, it's something to do with lactic acid build up. Luckily it was sunny and warm so we found a spot on the grass and I laid down, kicking off my trainers. It felt unbelievable to think I had completed something like that. It was unreal, but I had done it, and no one had even seen me cry. Coming back into the city, I had been hit by the reality of what I was doing, of how much I had changed and how much I had overcome. Big fat tears began to spill down my face, not because I was sad, but because I was so bloody proud of myself. I had pushed my body right to the edge in the way I had treated it, and yet it had bounced back stronger than ever and allowed me to run a whole half marathon. I almost couldn't believe it. I pulled my sunglasses down over my eyes and carried on running. It was hard. I couldn't catch my breath, but I was afraid someone would see me and think something was wrong. It really wasn't. I was better than I had been in a very long time.

After I stopped drinking I realised how little care I had taken of myself over the years. It was all the little things really, but it was easier not to do things, as I would have rather been at home with a glass of wine. Over the months things started to change. Lee must have thought the same because he started buying me simple but thoughtful gifts, face creams, nice towels that were just for me, encouraging me to take long baths. It was lovely, and gradually I began to remember what it was like to look after myself properly. I'd also got into a bad habit over closing one eye when I was tired and needed to read, because I hadn't been to the opticians in years. Having one eye which was weaker than the other meant I could get by without my glasses, and I didn't like wearing them. I was also afraid in my old job that due to the kids natures, they might get broken and I'd be without them so one day I stopped wearing them. Of course, I had a few headaches, but alcohol numbed that along with everything else, so it wasn't until I stopped drinking that I began to pay attention to how bad things were. So I trundled off to the opticians and was promptly told off for my poor vision and the fact that I drove without glasses. To be honest I hadn't realised it was that bad. It was a relief to get my glasses and to be able to see again, but if anything it did make me realise how bad my eyesight was without my glasses. Being outdoors in all weathers was great but I didn't like wearing my glasses when I ran, I didn't like the rain sticking to them and making it hard to see, and I was also scared that I would hurt myself or damage them if I fell over. I'd drive somewhere to run, take them off and then barely be able to see where I was going which was frustrating! Even in the evening, I felt a bit claustrophobic almost, having them on my face. I know loads of people wear glasses without problems, but I was sick of feeling restricted or reliant on something. Years before I had looked into laser surgery, but put myself off, thinking it sounded pretty scary. Then scrolling through social media one day, I saw another advert and before I could think too much about it, I booked myself a consultation appointment. They say something like one in four people aren't suitable for laser eye surgery, so I didn't hold out much hope, but to my surprise, I could have it done, and it would even correct the astigmatism I had in one eye. The problem was, thinking about the procedure itself just made me feel awful. I decided to put it out of my mind and ask them not to tell me too much about it, as I still had to meet the surgeon. I just kept telling myself that thousands of other people had done it before, and I couldn't be the only one who was nervous.

Meeting the surgeon was strange. I had to drive to a clinic two hours away, it seems that the surgeon moves between clinics rather than keep each one open all week. It sounds silly, but I even found that reassuring, that they had one really good surgeon who catered for lots of different areas. I'd also been reassured that he was a typical surgeon, and told he was 'an alpha male' who would apparently only do my surgery if he was sure he could achieve good results. So far he had a 100% success rate and he wouldn't jeopardise that at all by attempting a surgery that was more risky than usual. I tried to relax, and explained my worries to him, but he was very matter of fact, he told me that I had two options, one was to forget all about the surgery and not go through with it, while the second was to take diazepam for the day to relax me. I was pretty surprised that he would suggest that, as it seemed quite serious, but at the same point I wondered if it would help. Since he had suggested it I thought it might be worth a go. I only had a week between the meeting and the actual surgery, so I phoned the local surgery to make an appointment with the doctor. Of course there were no appointments available for over a week so I explained to the receptionist what I wanted and why, and once I had provided proof of the surgery the doctor was able to prescribe it over the phone for me. The prescription itself wasn't something I particularly wanted, but thought I'd get in case I really needed it, like a backup. Once I thought more about getting it though, it was like I couldn't relax until I had it. I'd virtually convinced myself that I wouldn't be able to have the surgery if I didn't have the tablets to relax me. I get like that, I was like it before with wine, I had to have more than enough otherwise I worry. Once it was in my hand, I felt better. It didn't matter if I took it or not, it just meant that it was there so I could take it if I needed to. Of course, I still wasn't sure if I would take the tablets, I remembered all the reasons I didn't like to take things like it, I wondered whether it would affect me adversely or if it would affect my sobriety. It was all a bit much to be honest. As was worrying about the surgery itself. I tried to put it out of my mind, but with only a few days left until my surgery, it was always on my mind. Lots of things were there to remind me, like the rules regarding makeup. I don't wear a lot in general, only really eyeliner and mascara, but I wasn't allowed to wear anything near my eyes for a few days before and several weeks after the surgery. It made me feel pretty self-conscious and almost naked in a way, but I knew it was for the best, so followed the rules to a tee. I'd heard enough scare stories to make me do everything I could to ensure I didn't have any problems.

One day before the surgery I had a race, a 10k trail run with Barn. We'd been looking forward to it for months, and due to one of the many severe storms we had throughout the autumn it had been postponed due to flooding on the course. Given that the date was moved so close to my surgery I was even more nervous than usual about running that morning. I had to drive an hour to get there, and once there removed my glasses to run, which made my eyesight even more blurry. The rain had stopped, but the course was very flooded, we were told that parts of it had been diverted, but at others we would have to run through standing water that was more than knee high. With a laugh it was added that it had gone down an awful lot! I was so nervous of getting something in my eye, or falling and hurting myself and not being able to have the surgery. It was also going to be the last time for several weeks that I could even run, as advice was I stopped that too until I was recovered. I decided to just run and enjoy it. Barn sped off into the distance, and I didn't. I enjoyed making my way through the woods, even if it was terribly slippery. I slowed down to enjoy the view as we ran over the cliffs, and I counted myself lucky that I wasn't one of the runners I passed that had to stop as they had an injury. We ran across the beach, up the cliff and back into the woods before coming back to the other side of the lake. It was much drier this side, but I was still very conscious that there were a lot of flies around! At one point, not far from the start, once we had navigated the woods and the mud, the path literally disappeared where the lake had swelled, and there was no choice but to run through it. It was so cold! Not being able to see the bottom was difficult as I wasn't sure where I was going to put my feet, but it was okay. I was happy I didn't end up swimming as I had my phone and car key in my pocket. I try to carry as little as possible, but sometimes I still have more than I'd like! The year before, the same race had been my first ever 10k, and I was hoping to beat my time, but given the circumstances, I was just pleased to finish it, and to enjoy it.

Monday morning came around and Lee drove me to my appointment. I didn't tell anyone else about the surgery, other than the kids, as I didn't want any well-meaning advice, or anything that could put me off, and I didn't want anyone to know if I decided I couldn't do it. It was expensive and I didn't want anyone's views on that even though I'm sure they wouldn't have commented or known if I'd spent the same amount on glasses or contact lenses! I still wasn't sure about taking the diazepam, but as Lee drove me to the appointment, it was over an hour and a half away, we talked about it, and he reassured me that he thought taking the diazepam on this occasion would be okay. I was pleased I did actually, and having the time to analyse myself I realised that times when I began to panic, which I often do in the car for some reason, instead of letting the feelings run away with me like I was used to, I managed to keep a hold on them and pull it back. It was really interesting to experience it that way, and although I felt calm, I didn't feel woozy or anything else. I felt like me, just a bit more relaxed. The wait was longer than normal, and then I was more grateful I had taken the tablets. It sounded like there was a problem with the parking and many of the surgical staff couldn't get into the building. I would have been a bundle of nerves normally, and although I can't say it was my favourite place to be, I felt okay. Every time I began to panic, I could get a hold of myself and calm myself down again. It made me think again about medication for my anxiety, whether it might be available, and whether it would make a difference to me. At the time though, I put those thoughts to one side, I had plenty of other things to think about right then.

The procedure itself was over quickly, and I was soon back in the recovery room. It wasn't the nicest thing ever, in fact there are a lot of other things I would prefer to do, and if I think about it now, it makes me feel squeamish, but the moment I sat up I could see better, and so it was worth it. I was discharged and Lee drove me home, but I hadn't been expecting it to be so bright. I'd been told to take sunglasses, but they just didn't cut it, and I ended up with my scarf wrapped around my head for the majority of the journey. I went to bed as soon as I got home, crawling up the stairs with my eyes closed. Lee hung a blanket over the curtains to darken it more for me. My eyes stung like I'd put raw onions in them and all I wanted to do was rub them fiercely, but of course I wasn't allowed, so I did as I was told and tried to sleep with my special protective goggles on. One by one the kids came home, and Katie came in to see me. She was afraid she was disturbing me, but it was nice to have the company and I told her that as long as she didn't mind me having my eyes closed, I was more than happy to talk to her. Gradually, I tried to open my eyes, which was hard as each time I did, water came gushing out and they stung and itched like crazy, but I realised I could read the alarm clock at the end of our bed, which I had never been able to do before. It was amazing, and as the days went by, my eyesight just got better and better.

The more I think about it now, the more I realise that I would never have been able to go through the surgery, the stress of the run up to it, and deal with the aftercare of it so well if I had still been drinking. The importance of correctly timing the four separate sets of eye drops I had been given and getting them in the right order was vital. I wouldn't have had the clarity of mind, and the ability to think things through so well before. It probably sounds naive but I hadn't imagined how many different areas of my life my sobriety would affect.

My third Christmas came and it was a lot easier than the year before. And even more easy than the year before that. Three alcohol free Christmases. That's something to be proud of isn't it? We spent the day at home, us and the kids, as is our tradition.

Then we see family on Christmas Eve or Boxing Day. It's only our parents who live near us, everyone else is hundreds of miles away so we aren't torn in too many directions like some people are. Work had been hectic, and working not only with Lee, but also his mum and dad and our eldest son Joe meant none of us really had time to prepare for anything until the last minute. I ended up doing the shopping for our kids from their Grandparents, choosing what they would want to help out, but instead of feeling put upon, I felt happy to help. We were busy right up until closing time on Christmas Eve. Then we all stopped.

Christmas Day was lovely. We were all tired, and Stanley was fighting off a bug, he always seems to get poorly around Christmas, but just spending time together was wonderful and for once, my thoughts didn't revolve around drink. I had one moment, where I felt a little lost, but it was over so quickly that I didn't even bother to say anything. I was standing by the fridge, and suddenly found myself reminiscing slightly about the thought of that glass. Of course my Christmases always involved wine. I remembered as clear as day, the feeling of the glass in my hand and the taste of the wine, that no other drink quite matched... And then I caught myself. That moment of sadness where I remembered I couldn't drink 'normally' like other people passed, and I moved on. Even these moments are becoming fewer and further between. I used to think they'd never stop and slowly they are, even if now they come out of the blue and surprise me. We had bought a new version of Monopoly, a game we had always enjoyed but seldom had the patience for. This year we played and no one got bored, upset or angry. Including me.

On Christmas Day I was so positive, but Boxing Day was a bit of a different story. It's weird how it catches you out. You get a bit complacent. You think you're fixed. At least I do. Or did. I've realised I'm not quite there yet. My mother and father in law were planning to come around, some years we go to them, and some years they come to us. In theory, everything should have been fine, I didn't really have a reason to find a problem with any of the arrangements and there was no pressure. They know I don't drink and have been totally supportive, but suddenly, about ten minutes before they arrived I started to panic. Over the years my mother in law and I shared quite a few bottles of wine. She is not a heavy drinker so I always drank more, but seeing them was always a reason to have few glasses. Reminding myself of that made me so envious, and I really wanted to be back there enjoying it even though it's been such a long time. I surprised myself standing by the fridge and remembering, wishing that a bottle would materialise in there for me. It's scary how things can still get to you after all that time. But the difference is now I can talk about it and tell Lee I'm struggling. Sometimes he's surprised, but if it catches me out, it's going to catch him out, he doesn't live in my crazy brain where I sometimes have a stupidly romantic idea of wine. That's all it is now though, I remember that although the picture would be nice, maybe sipping a nice glass of white at a bar overlooking a harbour, the reality would be more than a glass, more than a bottle or two probably. I wouldn't remember. I'd have a hangover. It wouldn't be fun. It would be sad and depressing and I know now, that however tempting it is sometimes, it is far better not to give in and to keep going in the direction I am.

It's strange how when you reminisce, you remember just the good and not the bad. You forget how one drink wouldn't be enough, and by the end of the evening you'd either be asleep, have embarrassed yourself or had an argument, or maybe all three. At least I probably would have. So, I had a little cry, reminded myself that it's my choice not to drink and that choice makes me a better person than the one I was. We put our shoes on and took the kids for a walk. It was tipping down and we got completely soaked but when we got back I felt so much better. My mind felt like it was my own again, and I'd been able to put off the temporary hijack from unwanted thoughts. I guess there are always going to be different triggers depending on what situations we face. Wine was involved in so much of my life, learning how to deal with each obstacle as they come up is going to take some time. So we got home, got dry and got out the Monopoly board, so the kids could try to beat their grandparents.

I notice the little things much more now, and I have more patience than I did before when I was drinking, to see the small things and let other things go. It was lovely as Lee had bought me a jigsaw puzzle as one of my presents, and Joe sat down with me for a minute to help me. It was so hard, a double sided puzzle of pigs in blankets with pieces that all look the same! I know Joe's main reason for doing it was because he wanted to go out again and was probably hoping that by giving me five minutes I'd let him go, but it was nice anyway. It was lovely to think he cares enough to do something like that with me, even if only for a few minutes, and instead of wasting time thinking about him going out, I just enjoyed the time we had.

That patience is something I am so grateful for, I feel him growing up and away and it is frustrating to think I can't really keep him here, that I don't see him very much and when I do, his head is often in his phone, but I try to be grateful for what I can get. I'm grateful that I have the time I do with them, and I'm grateful for the relationship I have with each of them. I'm working on being patient more, but I do find it hard sometimes. There is so much going on in my head that it makes me anxious before I've thought about anything else. Hearing the kids all chattering away at once just makes it harder to focus. I don't think I can be the only one, but it can be hard. So I'm reminding myself to relax, and be grateful. They grow up too fast, at 19, 17, 15 and 3, I know I have a few more years with them, but realistically, them moving out might not be too far away as Lee and I were already married and we had Joe when I was 19. I try to give them their freedom, I don't want them to feel like I'm clingy and that they have to stay at home with me all the time but it is nice when they want to. The things we do together are special.

I think that (smallest person aside) having the three of them so close in age, meant I was always physically and mentally tied up, and now that they are largely self-sufficient I have to adapt, and it's strange. I like the bustle of a busy house, I like them being about. I know my little man will be around for a lot longer and I am grateful for that, he is such a little bundle of fun, but it is strange knowing the others not needing me so much. Even Stanley is becoming much more independent.

On separate occasions while I was trying to address my drinking we went to my parent's house, both times for a meal. It was hard for me as I didn't really want to go out, it was difficult not to associate eating out with drinking, and evenings at my parents house had always involved a fair few glasses of wine. It was how they relaxed too. For a time neither of my parents really understood my drinking was a problem, although they seem to now. It must be hard for them, because unless you've experienced an addiction, you can't really see how hard it is for someone else. I'd tried to be upfront with them and at one point had actually been told to "pull myself together" which was hard. I was also told to moderate, but that was never an option for me. Once I'd had one glass it was too much. One Christmas when we were there we were invited in and asked to sit down. If I'd been drinking I would have been offered a glass as soon as I got through the door, but instead it was almost forgotten. A similar thing had been happening at Lee's Mum and Dad's too. It was almost like they forgot I might want a drink when I didn't want to drink alcohol. At Mum and Dad's though, they left us in the lounge to check on dinner and Dad soon popped back to offer us drinks offering me milk with a laugh. I know it was probably meant as a joke, and they were probably unsure really of what to do say, but I find comments like that really hurtful, it's almost as bad as telling me I am clearly boring for not wanting alcohol. The next year when we went, I was told there was wine on the table with the dinner. At this point I have to admit I laughed and did remind them I was an alcoholic so didn't drink. It was after I'd had the conversations with the kids and they knew, so I didn't have to be so careful about what I said. I was surprised though, because my parents seemed surprised! They were genuinely shocked that my status as an alcoholic who did not drink, literally meant that I didn't drink alcohol at all. They even questioned me, seeming surprised that I wouldn't drink with my meal, suggesting that it was all right because it was with food. I had to reassure them that for me, no alcohol quite literally meant no alcohol.

CHAPTER 13
2020

Depending on who you talk to and their perspective on recovery, it seems you might occasionally still encounter triggers. I know even after three and a half years of sobriety, I did. It's like there are things I thought I dealt with that I didn't and they catch me out. They make me remember.

A few years ago I felt like I could do anything. Nothing seemed to worry me, nothing seemed to get to me. Alcohol gave me an armour that took the edge off. If I worried about things more often than not, a glass of wine would help fix it. I never drank in the day, but more often than not, the after effects of the evening before helped take the harsh reality of tricky situations away, and at the end of the day would stop me overthinking. Somehow I could push through most things, but in hindsight, it was like I wasn't really there, it was like a game that I was watching but didn't really matter too much.

Of course I don't have that buffer of my feelings now. It makes doing things just a little bit harder as I have to face up to them head-on. The lack of a buffer really knocked me, I didn't realise how much harder things would be, and how things that seemed easy before, things that I could do with my eyes closed would be difficult. It became easier to stop doing a lot, at least the things I didn't have to do. I found my self-confidence plummeted and probably because I didn't push myself out of my comfort zone, things got worse.

I worried I would get things wrong, I was worried I would make a fool of myself, and in worrying, I stopped doing. I'm not sure what has changed, but something has, maybe it's just an element of time helping to heal? In the last few months I've started trying to do things again. I've tackled things a little more head-on. I started going out to business meetings again, something I really couldn't have faced a few months ago, but the more I do it, the easier it seems. I might not be the most confident speaker, addressing the room makes me nervous and I stumble a little over my words, but I know that I am an authentic version of myself, one that might make mistakes but is doing her best, and actually beginning to enjoy meeting people and getting things done again.

At the beginning of the year I attended a breakfast meeting. Being there for 7.30am wasn't something I would have looked forward to before, I would have struggled or felt groggy and to be honest it was hard leaving my warm bed, but I went anyway. Once I was on the road watching the sun break through the dark it was fine, as was the meeting. In fact it was more than fine, I spoke with lots of people, I addressed the room and didn't forget what I was saying. I laughed and enjoyed myself. The meeting was chaired by the CEO of the company, one who had run several businesses and had a lot of experience. He had suggested raising money for a local hospice and everyone had been supportive, so when he had asked for suggestions, he got a lot. It was decided that he wouldn't shave his beard until he reached £1000. This target was reached very quickly, because his wife wasn't keen on facial hair, and the month of charity fundraising could have been over, so he decided to go for a second target, again asking for suggestions. This time it was agreed that he would have to attend a days worth of meetings in drag if he could raise £2000. The temptation for a lot of us was too much and so that target too was surpassed and during this meeting he arrived looking like Freddy Mercury in the music video from "I want to break free." He looked stunning, and had a false name for the day too. It was fun to see him still chairing the meeting, but in such an unusual way. After the meeting I had a photo taken with my friend in drag and when I showed my daughter later, she said, "Mum you look so happy!" That she could see how I felt and that it was genuine means a lot.

A year ago you couldn't have paid me to go into a room full of people and pitch. But the more I did it, the better I felt about doing it, even if it does involve a little mental preparation beforehand. So I started to go to more and more, and began to relax about it. I began to see more and more familiar faces mixed in with the new faces that I didn't recognise. After each meeting people were encouraged to mingle and I got talking to someone I've met before a few times and chatted with. We spoke of work, Christmas, all sorts, and somehow got onto mental health and I may have said how much running helps me. Then we were talking about drinking, and without thinking I just said, 'I don't drink anymore.' I've said that before, but usually without the 'anymore' on the end, as it stops people asking any more questions. My colleague remarked how easy it could be to come to rely on it, how one drink turns into more, and I said I stopped over three years ago for that very reason. It was enough. I didn't have to explain, although as we talked more I did say how hard stopping had been. I felt accepted for being me, and not judged in the way

I had been fearing. It was refreshing and a lovely way to start the day. It gives me hope to feel I am moving on. Even sitting here thinking about it now, I actually feel proud of myself for admitting it to someone. All the little things add up. You might not see at the time, but gradually you realise how much difference you are making to your outlook.

Not so long after last Christmas I had a meeting in a pub. It doesn't bother me now like I thought it would, for a long time I didn't think I would be able to or even want to go into a pub again. I mean, what would be the point if you aren't going to have a drink? Even six months previously it would have been too much but things do seem to change and like I said, I had to, there was no option of venue. It isn't the first time either as a couple of weeks beforehand, I went for a coffee in a pub with some colleagues. The thing was that was quite explicitly just mid-morning coffee. There was no risk of anyone ordering anything more than a hot drink so I knew what to expect, although of course someone made a joke about it not being too early for something stronger. This next one was a lunch meeting, and it was the first time I've done that since I stopped drinking. I didn't really think of it until just before, I assumed that because it was work no one would drink. But then I started to worry a bit, and that is frustrating because it isn't like I need to drink even if others are.

I managed to get a seat and seeing there were lots of bottles of water on the table I felt safer, so to speak. It wasn't long before a gentleman came in with another woman. Before they had even sat down they were announcing to the room that they were going to try to avoid drinking, especially as it was still

January (Dry January). He soon followed this by saying that the tonic waters they had just bought cost £4.50 so it would have been cheaper to drink alcohol. Then the conversation moved to how expensive drinking could be and the cost of various varieties of alcoholic drinks. I felt a bit uncomfortable as this wasn't a conversation I wanted to participate in, and yet I didn't want to be rude. No sooner had I thought this than another attendee joked loudly, "Boy, am I glad I don't drink anymore." I know this person also had a drinking problem in the past, but I had never heard them acknowledge it before, and I was pleasantly surprised. This comment was followed by, "Celebrating twelve years," to which I replied, "Wow, well done." I didn't like to say too much and yet I felt it deserved recognition, but where I was worried about drawing too much attention, this person just bravely said, "Well yeah, it was either give up, or die," which while serious, made me laugh, as was the intention. Without even really meaning to, I just said, "It's three years for me." It was the second time in a short space of time that I admitted to people outside of my circle the truth, and the minute it was out of my mouth, I wondered what I had done. I almost expected people to be staring, wondering whether I was contagious or something. But no one else seemed to react, maybe they just didn't care, but then why would they? My addiction and obsession with what others think of me shouldn't be the first and only thing that people think about when walking into a room. The person I was talking to congratulated me and the conversation in the room moved on, as it already was around us.

Later after the meeting, where I drank a lot of water and nothing else, the same person caught me and we chatted. Although we both knew of the other's troubles, we had never spoken to each other about it, only through my husband. We joked about how we wouldn't have been able to face being in a pub a while ago, but now neither of us were going to jump the bar to down a quick one. Then when talking about our other halves, my friend even said that their partner could take or leave it which would have been our downfall, we could take it but never leave it. "Who is sicker?" I was asked. Us, the drinkers, or them, the spouses? Them, I replied, to which my friend laughing out loud said, "Yes exactly, why would they put up with us and all the crap we've given them over the years? What is wrong with them?" It was funny to be so open about it, a relief to talk and not have to explain or be ashamed or embarrassed but just to laugh at the situation and our experiences in a lighthearted way. It was another experience I could tick off my list, one that is surprisingly no longer a trigger, but an experience I can enjoy if I want to.

Our 15 year old son Barn is sat his English GCSE last summer. To relieve pressure he did one early, and the rest next year and is the third of my four to sit these exams although the first to do it staggered over two years, so I know roughly what to expect, not that it made it any easier for him! Just before Christmas he came home to tell me there was a trip to the Theatre Royal in Plymouth to see one of the main plays in his syllabus, 'An Inspector Calls'. He was interested in going, but by the time I'd logged onto the school's online payment system not long after, all the available places had gone. He was disappointed, and me being me, I felt like I'd let him down by not getting him a place, even though there was little else I could do. Normally he wouldn't be that bothered about school trips so it made me feel worse that I hadn't been able to secure him a place on this one. I thought about it and suggested booking it separately and just the two of us going, I wasn't sure if he would want to go with me or not, but he was happy to, as long as we went on a different day to the rest of the school.

I'd forgotten I hadn't taken him to the theatre before. It's something I used to love, and I often used to go with some of my friends, but that was before, when an evening out involved a show, dinner and copious amounts of wine. I took my daughter a few years back to see Hairspray which was fun, but even then I was a little preoccupied with wanting to get home afterwards for a glass of wine. I was envious of those in the audience drinking, but couldn't as I had a thirty mile drive home, and was scared to risk it. At least I had some limits back then, I didn't drink when I was 'on duty' as a mum, and not at all when I was driving, but that didn't stop me wanting to. I always noticed what other people were drinking and felt envious of those who had something I didn't. It was easier not to go out than to face other people drinking, especially in the early days when it was all tinged with a fair bit of jealousy and the feeling you are missing out on something special. When you get into the habit of going home straight after work and staying in all evening, it sticks and it takes quite a lot of hard work to change your habits. It's scary, and pushes you out of your comfort zone, which is hard when you're already feeling on edge. I've had to relearn a lot of routines and behaviours. I've had to acknowledge and sit with feelings I didn't even know I had. It's not all bad though. It's just new.

Although I was looking forward to going out with Barn, I still had that familiar pull reminding me that it would easier to stay at home. I worried that I would be tired in the morning for work, I worried that I would be too tired to make the drive home. But, as I try to do, I pushed myself and it was great. As I said, Barn had never been before and it was lovely to enjoy the experience with him. He was surprised at how big the theatre was, and hadn't see a live performance like that before so it was all quite an experience for him. I did let him down a bit though, only in that I'd promised him ice cream in the interval, and there wasn't one.

I've read a couple of books by a writer called Jen Sincero. In one she said, "When you change who you're being, you're basically killing off your old identity, which completely freaks your subconscious out." It's true. It takes time to change, and you're fighting against all your ingrained and learned habits that have been with you for years. Before, I always used to feel rushed to get home. I knew that waiting for me there was my familiar glass of wine. My reward at the end of the day. Things do change and although it has taken a lot of time, finally some things seem to be getting a little easier.

I often, although not as often as I used to, get a fleeting panic when it's getting late at work or I'm out late in the evening. I feel like I should be rushing home, but when I catch myself and stop for a breath I realise I have no reason for it. I used to worry about early mornings or late afternoon appointments because they might have affected my plans. Now, they don't. I can pretty much do what I want to do and there's no hangover or residual alcohol left hanging around upsetting things. There are be ups and downs, but it does get easier.

I try really hard to be honest in my writing, I am not on a mission to convert everyone in the world to sobriety, but I am trying to prove that life without alcohol is good. For those of us who choose it anyway. I struggled for a long time to admit I had a problem and to do anything about it because I was so scared I wouldn't be able to cope without it. The fear of missing out was huge, and as I have said before, our society does nothing to help that, everywhere you look alcohol is used as a remedy to fix just about every emotion or situation. So since I've worked out that wine is not a prerequisite to a good life, I want to shout it out to anyone who will listen, because there might be one person out there that reads it and thinks, "Okay, maybe I could do it." That's the sort of support I needed, so I want to be there for others if I can. I know I can be over-sensitive; I know I over think, but sometimes comments that seem flippant to one person can really hurt another person and I've had a couple of comments recently that have upset me in all honesty. The surprising thing is that they haven't come from any of my readers but instead from people I'd expect more from really. Firstly someone close to me asked about my blog. It was the first time in quite a few months, so caught me by surprise. I am so proud of my writing and of being able to talk to everyone who reads it, as well as the lovely comments I get from so many people. I am also conscious that while it matters to me, I don't want to bore everyone in the 'real world' so I don't tend to say too much unless I am asked. Well, I answered honestly, and said that my following is growing and I really enjoy the conversations I have with everyone. I know social media and blogging is not for everyone, and clearly not for the person I spoke to, because the person kind of brushed it off, and instead of being proud of me or giving me words of encouragement, told me it didn't matter how many followers I had, as what really mattered was family. I know my family is important, I'm pretty vocal about how important my family is to me, and how I couldn't have got through this without Lee and the kids, but actually my writing is important too. At least it is to me. My blog was the first thing in a long time that I have done just for me, with no-one else's input. Sometimes I worry that I say too much, but I pride myself that what I write is honest and true if nothing else. It might sound a bit soft, but to be able to have something that I can do without looking for anyone else's approval makes me feel good, and to think that I am giving something back to the sobriety community makes me feel like I am doing something good too. I was a bit hurt that this person couldn't see that.

I'd expected negativity from out there, you know, from people I don't know, who don't get me, but from people I know it makes me question what I am doing and if it's wrong. But I just about shook it off. I try to be strong, and writing makes me feel good. It helps me work through how I feel, and actually helps me deal with the things I've been through. Before I might have got cross, it possibly might have ended in an argument, not everyone can understand how it feels to be in my situation and so they possibly could think that I misconstrued the comments. I know people in general, especially those close to me wouldn't intentionally try to hurt my feelings, but by trying to make me similar to them, they do. I don't drink because one glass for me would never be enough, and I don't want to go back there. I don't miss it, not now, and while I still get a little 'wine glass envy' occasionally, it is certainly more the romantic idea of it that I miss than the actual thing. I don't feel like I'm missing out either and it's taken me a long time to get to a point where I can say that. I don't need it to relax either and saying that feels fantastic. I feel strongly that those people who can go ahead and 'enjoy' one or two drinks and don't have a problem should feel free to, but please don't judge those of us who can't and no longer want to.

Especially when we are learning to be happy just the way we are. I was really upset after one conversation, but I really tried to put it to one side. I know it probably wasn't meant in the way it came across and while it seems that some seem to try to justify their drinking as a means of relaxation, by putting it into perspective, or at least what I assume might be their perspective, I can understand how they could feel. It might be that they are at the point that I was, when I couldn't see the point in life without wine, when I couldn't see how I could relax or have fun or enjoy myself without a few glasses. I have to try and remember that just because I don't drink, doesn't mean other people don't. And that's okay. As long as they don't try to change what I'm doing.

Like a lot of people I was shocked to hear of the sudden passing of TV presenter Caroline Flack in the spring of 2020. You didn't need to be a fan or even have liked her to be taken aback at what happened, and regardless of the issues she has had in the press, it has to be acknowledged that she was a young woman, with a family who cared about her and a life in front of her. It's deeply saddening to think for her it was all too much. Whenever I saw Caroline on TV I often thought she looked a bit fragile. She had a very good exterior, don't get me wrong, but there was something there that made me feel like she was similar to me. For a long time I was also good at projecting what I thought people wanted to see, and how I wanted to be perceived when I was shaking on the inside. I was a firm believer of the saying, "Fake it until you make it." I felt that if you could push through it would make it easier to do it next time, and the time after, until eventually it became second nature and you just did it without worrying. I wonder if Caroline was like that? I'm not sure, I don't know, and it isn't my place to know, but I do know that there was more there than met the eye. But then there often is with many people.

I think it is frustrating and saddening in the day and age we live in that there isn't more help for people that need it. Actually it makes me angry that there isn't. We are all super connected by the internet and social media and yet many of us are lonely. It makes no sense. Mental health is discussed and we are told to open up and talk about things, yet who is really there to listen? Our friends and family aren't qualified and can only do the best they can with the knowledge they have. I know that I asked for professional help over the years several times and didn't get what I needed. Waiting lists are often too long, and if you're like me, once you've been turned away one too many times, you take matters into your own hands and refuse to ask for help anymore. My approach doesn't help matters, in fact it probably just contributed to the isolation I felt. I just wonder, if I had proper help with my mental health when I had asked for it, if I might have got better sooner, rather than still be dealing with it now after years of self-medicating with alcohol. It takes a lot to ask for help though, and to be turned away knocks you at the very least, possibly making you feel like you're a time waster. I know I felt like that.

Addiction is not the same thing as suicide, but people aren't the same either. They each have their own experiences and their own ways of dealing with things. People adapt to their circumstances, and sometimes they stop adapting because they can't do it anymore. It seems like people are talking more now in the wake of Caroline's death about being kind, which I admire, and it would be amazing if something good could come from something so sad. I wonder though really, how much will change.

It sounds cynical, but what difference will it really make? For real change, we need to educate our children more, to be kind and accepting, but at the very least to tolerate difference. Teenagers can be particularly unkind if someone doesn't fit in, and often it is just due to a lack of understanding, rather than an innate unkindness or need to be hurtful. Nothing will change overnight, and the problem is, no one thinks it will happen to them, or to their friend, until it does. And then it is often too late.

I hope that the hashtag of the moment will encourage more kindness, and that everyone will in general #bekind to each other. No one knows what is going on behind closed doors, or behind a carefully constructed mask. Often the most vulnerable people are the ones most likely to put up a convincing act. It doesn't mean they are strong, it just means they are good at hiding their weakness. But because of this, it is often these people that are missed, because they look okay to the outside world. Maybe we can just try to remember that when we go about our daily lives. Just to look a bit closer sometimes and not assume. Maybe we can stop for a second and ask if someone is okay, and actually listen to them when they tell us? Maybe I'm hoping for too much? It's just my thoughts after all. I think too, that for anyone vulnerable to accept help, we need to be approached at the right time by the right person. They need somehow to spy that chink in our armour or it won't work. We've often spent many years perfecting that suit of armour and it's hard to let it down once it is up.

Back to running... In February I ran my first half marathon of the year, it was a hilly one and beforehand I felt very nervous. This time last year I hadn't run a half marathon at all. The furthest I had run was 10k which is just over six miles, but then over the course of the year I ran four half marathons, Plymouth, Eden, Cornwall Coast to Coast, and one at Cardinham woods which was ridiculously hilly. They were all varied, but my times were pretty consistent, and I enjoyed them, so you'd think I'd feel okay about running another one. Instead, doubt crept in. With the last one being over five months ago, it's long enough to for me to begin to think I can't do it anymore. Then, as if I needed more excuses, which I don't, (I think the years of making excuses for my drinking have made me a pro at it), I had a bad chest, which got better, but was a bit nasty for a minute so affected my training a bit, although I was grateful it wasn't as bad as last year, when I had pleurisy after a chest infection. Then there has been the weather. It had been atrocious. Not that it's an excuse, I know I can still run in bad weather, I know I am waterproof, but, you know, it's easier not to sometimes. So my long runs, weren't really been long enough for the training I should have been doing. I kept telling myself I would be fine and yet that doubt just niggling away at me.

Our local parkrun events are never cancelled, and yet in the face of Storm Dennis, which followed on from Storm Ciara the weekend before, they were. It's not ideal to be running in such wooded areas with high winds and rain, so I totally understand, but given that the half I was running was to be held at the same National Trust estate as my local parkrun, I sort of assumed it would be cancelled too. I'd allowed myself to believe it would be, but of course, because I tempted fate, it wasn't and although I was nervous, I was feeling excited too. I didn't particularly want to get drenched or blown away, nor did I want to admit defeat, and knowing there was a cut off time did nothing for my nerves! The cut off was an hour longer than the other half's I've run and yet knowing it is there does me no good. I feel like I could fail before I begin.

As it was so local didn't have to be up too early which was a nice bonus, although parking could be interesting so we gave ourselves a few extra minutes. I wasn't sure that I'd be much use driving home afterwards as my legs tend to get a bit stiff, so Lee drove me down. But registration was fine, and done quickly so we then had about 45 minutes before the start. I planned that if the weather was totally horrendous in the morning, I could change my mind and just not go. I knew I wouldn't, to me it would feel like giving up, but having a back up plan was quite nice. Barn was still too young to run that distance, but he told me he'd join me for some moral support at a few points, he's quite good at it on races he isn't allowed to join in with yet. Seeing the weather, I wasn't sure that he would come, and I left him in bed, knowing he would easily be able to catch me up if he came down on his bike. Twice he has run the same ten miler with me just to keep me company as he was too young to run it properly. The frustrating thing is how easy he makes it look! I try to stay positive though, because I know besides my doubts, my body often runs better than my mind thinks it can.

At the start there was a lot of bustling about, a sports hall full of runners and I only recognised a few faces. The organisers had been very clear about the inability to do any last minute transfers, but I think given the weather and Storm Dennis, quite a few people had been unable to travel to the race, so they were able to make a few last minute amendments to the entries. The race had filled up very quickly so it was lovely to see some of those that had been unable to get a place being able to run at the last minute. The weather was shocking, but I guess, with all the weather warnings, at least we were expecting it, and it didn't just come out of no-where. We were running through Storm Dennis after all! I was most impressed with the man running in only a vest, shorts and sandals. I would have been freezing! To be fair, I was pretty cold anyway! I suppose, it's probably better to run in less, at least your skin doesn't hold weight like wet clothes!

The race itself was lovely. Running through some cycle paths from the start to our local National Trust property was nice in itself but quite protected. Once we got down to the forest, it was apparent how wet and rainy it was, the river looked ready to burst its banks, but it was great to have a reason to be out in the elements, rather than staying indoors and looking out at it. It was two laps which was hard, and unexpected, especially as when I was coming to the end of my first lap I was passed by the front runners coming to the end of their race. That was a bit disheartening, and I think that because of the weather, quite a few runners hadn't arrived. It was quite noticeable that there were a lot of elite fast runners, but not many of the gently paced runners or plodders. Without the mix of runners, being near the rear of the pack was unusual, but none of us were going particularly slowly. It was quite strange. At the end of that lap I found my Barn waiting for me on his bike. He was soaked through but it was good to see him. He rode alongside me for a lot of the rest of the race, it's one of those things I always feel a little bit envious about, other people having company when I don't. It can be quite lonely running for over 13 miles without anyone to chat to. Not that I have the breath spare to chat a lot! I guess this is the advantage of joining a local running club where you can run with friends.

My little voice of doubt was certainly there beforehand, but strangely as I ran I seemed to leave it behind. I think the wildness of the weather helped distract me, as did the hills and the mud that was terribly slippery. But it was good fun. In the last mile I struggled, my legs were cold and I wondered if I could finish, but I did, maybe it was a second wind, or maybe I just ran through the doubt? Either way, I got to the finish line and I wasn't last. It wasn't my best time, but given the conditions, I was pretty happy with it.

In March I ran the biggest race I have ever run. Not the longest because I've run a few half marathons now, but definitely the biggest. I posted on my blog the night before we went, worrying and had so much support that I felt I had to go because if I didn't I wouldn't just be letting myself down, but also all the wonderful people who encouraged me.

This year I wanted to run the London Marathon, I've never run anything that long but I got excited about it watching last years on the TV and thought it would be a good goal to set for myself. I entered the ballot and although I had a really good feeling about it, I didn't get a place so I entered the London Landmarks Half. I didn't get a place in that ballot either, so I was a bit more disappointed, but when I saw the Vitality Big Half being advertised without a ballot I bought a place straightaway. As we live in Cornwall I was hoping to book a hotel and have a few nice days away. It seemed like such a good idea, but being busy things got in the way and I didn't really plan as much as I would like. I ended up almost ignoring it as the thought of it worried me and as it got closer to the event, it all seemed a bit much. It was more of a mission than I intended it to be, hotels were booked up already, didn't have parking or too far away and I saw little point in booking somewhere to stay if we were going to have to leave so early we wouldn't be able to have breakfast. Panic attacks were still affecting me and the thought of sitting in the car for such a long way scared me so I almost decided not to go. Looking at the website to see if I could defer until the following year I saw The Little Half being advertised, a 2.3 mile event on the same day suitable for under 18's and those not able to run the full half. Seeing such a unique opportunity for the kids, I decided to book Katie and Barn onto that too, hoping it would at least give them something to look forward to, rather than just being there to watch me. It also gave me more incentive not to cancel and to push myself to go as it was no longer just going to be me who would miss out. Most of the races I've done are small, local events, the biggest was my first half marathon in Plymouth where there were about five thousand runners. Running the Vitality Big Half in London there were over twenty thousand. I've never run something with so many people before, and I've never had to start in a wave before either. That was strange, but weirdly reassuring, knowing most of the people around me were a similar speed to me, based on the predicted times we'd put down. It was a lot to take in and organise and we decided in our wisdom to do the trip in one day. We looked and looked for the best underground option too, because many of the stations we'd used on previous trips were shut due to maintenance, which I couldn't believe considering the amount of additional people travelling to the capital for the race. It made the planning harder, but we thought we would work it out.

That Sunday morning we got up at 2am, my Joe had gone clubbing so decided not to come with us as he stayed with friends, just leaving the three younger kiddies. Trying to keep the littlest man asleep we got into the car, aiming to be at Ruislip for just after 6am. When we got there, we realised I'd misread the stations and Ruislip was another one of the stations that was shut, we were supposed to be at West Ruislip instead! We'd already parked the car, and so a very kind bus driver let us on and dropped us off at the right station. It was an extra thing I didn't need. I'd managed to make it through the journey without worrying too much. I'd only had two or three head between my knees and try to breathe moments, so was doing pretty well considering. Anxiety gets me at the strangest times, even when I know that logically I am okay, it just comes out of no-where. It was a huge relief when I saw other runners carrying their marked kit bags for the race as I knew I wasn't going to be the last runner to arrive, at least while I could see them! That helped me to relax, as did the enjoyment our two year old had at seeing and riding on the trains. He was so excited bless him, we've only brought him to London once before that, and he was so small then he wouldn't have remembered it.

Forty minutes after we got on that train we jumped off to change over, and obviously having traveled a long way, needed the toilet. Many of the stations have closed the facilities they did have, which is fine if you're local, but isn't so good when you've come so far and don't know where to go! An attendant pointed us out in the direction of the public toilets, and when we got there we realised we needed change to pay. That was brilliant, I'd left my purse at home which I never do, but wanted to carry less as I would be leaving the majority of it with Lee and he had only brought cards with him. We had no choice but to turn back, but the idea of being stuck on a train again, with no idea where the nearest toilets would be worried us, but at least it wasn't just me for a change! Seeing a cafe, I asked the owner if we could use their facilities, and he kindly let us, despite not even being open yet. I wouldn't normally have the nerve to ask, but I was so glad I did because by the time I got to the start of the race, although there were many portaloos, there were queues of ten to twenty people for each one. I had no chance of getting in there! Going back to catch our next train, poor Katie tripped and fell, banging her hip, shoulder and shin on the metal edged steps in the underground, which really hurt, but also embarrassed her, we were so lucky it wasn't worse or it could have really spoiled the day for her. I guess that's what you get for rushing!

We literally got to Tower Hill one minute before my wave loading closed. I panicked, thinking they wouldn't let me in, and dropped all my extra stuff on the pavement for Lee and the kids, before running to the start following the correctly coloured arrows. I had no idea where I was going, but marshals directed me according to my colour and number of my wave. The panic of getting there on time, and the concentration I needed to find where I was going probably helped me as I had something to focus on doing. And then I was there. Standing. It was so weird. There were hundreds of us, just waiting. In the distance I could see Tower Bridge, and a massive screen showing the elite runners who had started much earlier just flying along, making it look so effortless. I took a photo and posted it on my blog, wanting everyone to know how much the encouragement they had given meant to me and that I was there, ready to go. Lee and I texted a few times, he wanted me to know he was there, which was reassuring, but we didn't manage to see each other. In the distance we could hear counting down and we began to move forward. Another wave started and we moved forward again. Soon enough we were there at the start, well the front of my wave was, I couldn't see it! And then, we were off.

Mostly the half marathons I've done are hilly being as I live in Cornwall which means I give myself the excuse to run and walk the steep bits if I need to. It helps break it up, and in my head feels like a break, even if I don't stop. Not so in London. It was so flat! I had no choice but to run all but a couple of steps at the water stations. It was great to show me that I really could do it, as I am so used to slowing down, before the race itself I did begin to question whether I could run the full distance again. As we ran, we moved through the different districts of London and it was so amazing to see the different performances they had put on for us. There were samba bands, brass bands, choirs, all kinds, the support was brilliant. We ran through the longest tunnel, which upset my Garmin and told me that I was half a mile ahead of where I thought I was. I overtook the Eiffel Tower and a Rhino, and a bunch of grapes, among other people running, and it was fantastic.

The organisers had also suggested good places for the spectators to watch our race would be, so I knew in all likelihood I wouldn't see Lee and the kids before mile seven or eight, but it was hard not knowing where they'd be. I kept watching and the further I went, I knew I was nearer to seeing them, and then the sights would take my attention again. The Little Half, which Katie and Barn were running started around my mile eleven and finished at the same point as me too. I hoped I'd be finished to see them run, but didn't know for sure, all I did know was that Lee would take them to the start if I didn't join them. My thoughts were interrupted again by the views, and running across Tower

Bridge was unbelievable. Something so iconic that I have walked across many times, and yet I got to run over, straight down the middle of the road, with people watching and cheering. It was fabulous. I felt very emotional, but I didn't cry. (Not like my first half, where I cried quite a lot!)

Mile nine came and went, and then ten, and I thought I'd probably missed my family, that they were probably getting ready for the start of their race. But then sometime around mile eleven, when I was beginning to struggle, I saw them all sitting on the pavement and watching out for me. It was so good to see them, such a boost, and perked me up for the finish. That last mile and a bit was the hardest. It seemed to go on forever, and after the incredible Tower Bridge nothing much was going to match up. But I kept going as best I could. Running on cobbles earlier had hurt my ankle a bit, and the wind was strong to run into. I was getting tired, but I had to finish, and in my head, the fact there wasn't a hill meant I couldn't walk. So I pushed on, and got to the finish line. It wasn't my fastest, but I am so proud of it. What an experience it was to run through such an amazing city.

It took nearly an hour for me to get out of the finish area. I heard a lot of people talking and I'm not sure what happened, as apparently the organisation was better in the previous year. I had no choice but to wait with everyone else, but it was cold, I couldn't get to my hoody, but then, neither could anyone else. They funnelled us all into a line which left the finish area to enter the festival area in Greenwich Park to collect our medals, fruit, t-shirt, and other goodies. We had to stop at one point as a runner was in a bad way and had to be brought through to an ambulance. Eventually I got through, and made my way back to the finish to see the kids, but I'd missed them running and they had already finished. Poor Lee was struggling along with all the bags and a toddler asleep on his shoulders, trying to get to the end to see us. It was a nightmare to track down the kids, as a lot of the streets had turned into single file, and if you weren't careful you could get carried along the wrong way. Eventually though I managed to find them and we decided to walk (I hobbled) back the two miles to meet Lee and Stanley.

It was a fab experience for the kids too, they've never run anything like it either, Katie was so proud, she ran the whole thing and really enjoyed it. I was especially proud of her because she had hurt herself earlier when she fell but still carried on. Barn flew, (again) coming in 4th place in the whole race, of almost 1300 runners. If he'd started at the front, he may have gained a few places, but he doesn't often like to and had started with his sister. The best bit was that they enjoyed it. It was such a shame I didn't get to see them run, or be there at the finish for them but Lee managed to get a video for me as they passed him.

It was a great day, a day I never would have experienced if I had still been drinking. I never would have been capable of running so far and wouldn't have coped well at all with the early start and late evening without a glass of wine or two. By the end of it my feet really hurt! I hadn't thought about the walk to and from the start really, and then going back to meet Lee was further again. Although I heard later that the station nearest the finish was packed so it would probably have taken even longer to get home had we done that. Although I worried about getting there, about even managing the car journey there, I proved to myself once again that I am capable of doing more than I think I can.

CHAPTER 14
DEALING WITH MY ANXIETY

The day after the race in London I saw the doctor about getting some help with my anxiety. A month or so before I finally gave in and admitted I needed some from someone beyond what I could do for myself. I've been doing everything I can by myself, but it's exhausting to keep having to fight my mind at every turn. It can be something insignificant, or just a change in situation, but my mind circles and worries and blows things out of proportion escalating to panic attacks at times. I've always been interested in alternative therapies and actually trained as a holistic therapist years ago. Since giving up alcohol, I've tried to employ all manner of alternative ways of defusing my anxiety and keeping my mind calm. You name it, I've tried it, mindfulness, yoga, meditation, oils, crystals, walking, running, everything. They all help a little, but nothing takes the edge off my busy mind like wine used to.

In all honesty, I should have gone a long time ago, but I still do struggle to trust doctors and always feel they won't believe me. Past experience has taught me that they don't always listen and they don't always help so I avoid them at all costs if I can. However, I had to see a physiotherapist again a few months ago who suggested I saw someone about my mental health. She could clearly see I was struggling and I hadn't expected her to. I didn't realise it was that obvious. She pointed out that I had a lot of coping strategies in place, and when they weren't there, I struggled more. It made sense, and sometimes however much I hate to admit it, when outsiders see things it makes it seem more real. I listened to her but dismissed her. This was after I'd ended up in tears because waiting out in the waiting room had been hard. I just about coped until my appointment time came and went and then my heart began to race. I can't pinpoint why I panic in certain situations, but they are very hard sometimes for me to deal with. On my next appointment she suggested it again, and again I thanked her and told her I was okay. She was keen for me to see someone, so I felt it was easier to discontinue my appointments with her. It wasn't the right thing to do, but I just wanted to bury my head in the sand. Not long after that, I had a phone call from the doctors surgery, asking me to make an appointment to follow up from a letter from the physio. I made the appointment, but cancelled it not long after, not wanting to waste it if someone else needed it. Of course I should have gone then. Having my eye surgery, and taking the diazepam which made such a difference to me that day made me begin to wonder if there was something out there that would be able to help me. Mind you, that was in November and it took me until March to get there.

I phoned and tried to make an appointment to see my doctor who was of course fully booked for the following two months. I explained to the receptionist about the physio referring me, and promptly burst into tears which I hadn't expected. It takes a lot for me to ask for help and I find it so hard, so it makes me emotional. Anyway, despite my apologies the poor receptionist then conjured up a new appointment for me. My doctor is lovely, and was really helpful towards the end of my drinking, she was the one who prescribed my Antabuse which helped me finally kick it. Although it was a way off, it was a relief having the appointment, but of course, as I do, I began to convince myself that I didn't really need it and that I was wasting her time. Usually I would have cancelled it, but this time I didn't. The night before, I was certain I should cancel it, but I still didn't. So I went. I waited for the doctor to tell me I was being silly, that I didn't need anything to help me along, that maybe it was all in my head. But she didn't. She listened and she seemed to understand.

I explained how things have been since I stopped drinking. How I am so much better, but I still have so far to go, that I don't want to worry about ridiculous things that aren't even going to happen, but it's like my mind needs to. That sometimes it runs away with me. She didn't judge and she didn't tell me I was silly. The doctor understood my worries and offered me a few options of things I could try. Apparently beta blockers can take away the physical symptoms of panic attacks, but I think now I've got a fairly good handle on that side of things, it's just my mind that is too busy. So she went through some others, all non-addictive ones, so I don't have to worry and then gave me a prescription. It was so nice to finally be heard. I've asked for help from the doctors over the years and always feel like I've been brushed off. People have told me to stop worrying but that doesn't work in the same way it didn't work when people told me to stop drinking. I told her that I no longer wanted to drink, and hadn't done so in over three years, but nothing quietened my mind like wine used to do. She listened, she didn't tell me to pull myself together or any of that rubbish and it made me feel better.

Being prescribed medication is not something I wanted, I even wondered if it would affect my sobriety and if I should let myself rely on something else, but actually, for the first time in a long time, I don't feel worried all the time, which is a huge bonus! My mind is much quieter, it's sort of peaceful and my emotions are levelled out more than they have been in a long time. It's quite nice.

I'm enjoying feeling the novelty of this calm, with the added benefit that because it isn't alcohol induced, it actually remains and I also remember. I feel balanced without the up and down rollercoaster of calm and stress that I experienced when I was drinking. So it's weird that my mind is already questioning whether I was ever bad enough for medication, in the same way I questioned when I was that bad when I was drinking. That doubt is annoying. I feel more able to listen to myself this time though, I sort of trust that I was that low, and actually, it's nice to be on a bit more of a level playing field for a change. I wasn't expecting wonders, and yet I can't remember the last time I felt this continually calm. I've had a few headaches, but if that is the only side effect, then it's fine by me. But it's been over nine months now and even those seem to have gone now. It's good to feel in control again, to not have my mind and my emotions run away with me. Even in more stressful situations, and by that I mean the things that a lot of people would take in their stride, I just feel able to stay on top, and that feels so good right now. My mind currently feels the most quiet it has in a long time. I can concentrate on the TV again or on reading, without my mind wandering off somewhere else. I still feel like me, just more relaxed. That's not to say I don't ever worry or panic, but I'm still human and I wouldn't want to be absent of all feelings. I guess I'll have to wait and see whether it works in the long term, but so far, so good!

As the days went on I carried on with my blog, finding the more I wrote the more I wanted to write. It seemed to help me untangle my mind, and work out my feelings as I encountered new things, or things that made me think. I carried on reading, even though I'm sober and have no intention of changing that, I find that even now, reading other people's experiences helps me. It makes me feel less alone, and part of a movement of people that no longer drink. It reinforced my feelings and gave me strength and made me feel less negative about my path so far. If you're like me and enjoy devouring books, you may have heard of Lotta Dann aka Mrs D. She's from New Zealand, and an author of several books about sobriety. She also has her own blog and like me, she is an advocate of living a sober life, hosting a great site called Living Sober. I was so honoured to be interviewed by Lotta when she asked me to talk about my sobriety, and how my life has improved since I stopped drinking. It was nerve wracking sharing the information, and although I was so proud and excited to do it, I was nervous of sharing it amongst people I knew to start with. Every positive reaction I got from anything posted online helped my confidence grow and my resilience come back a little.

CHAPTER 15
COVID-19

And then of course came Covid-19. It came out of the blue for most of us, and I for one thought it might be one of those things that is scary but stays on the periphery, never quite touching our lives as we expected it to, or worried it might, like the threats of Ebola and similar in the past. Of course this was different, it came fast and it didn't stop. It touched everyone, and it made me realise how truly grateful I am for my sobriety. We are, as I write this, coming to the end of our second lockdown in the UK. Having been through the first one in the spring, I know I certainly wouldn't be coping with the crisis if I was still drinking. I think in all honesty, I would be impossible to live with.

As a family we followed the guidelines and didn't stockpile, but as there are six of us living together, we did buy a few things that will last, in case the shelves once again become as bare as they were and also, in case one of us contracts the virus and we actually can't get out. Both sets of our parents were at home in self-isolation during the first lockdown and there is no-one else I would be able to ask to get things for us, so I've had to prepare us a little. I couldn't reasonably ask my parents to collect something for us, and live with myself if they got ill because of me. It makes me think how different it would be if I was still drinking and how I would have stockpiled for that. I can't quite get my head around how much wine I would have bought, how I would have excused it and where I would have put it. It would have cost a fortune! Given the queue to get into our supermarket some days, I would have spent a long time there, probably more than I do at home! I've even heard some countries banned alcohol entirely during the lockdown. That would have been unbearable for me and despite the fact that I can't see the UK going that far, I know it would have made me feel uneasy to think they could enforce it. I can't imagine not being able to get a drink if I needed one, and I know there will be some people out there who find themselves in that situation.

One of the many reasons I began to address my drinking problem all that time ago was because I began to worry about the amount I had to buy, not only to drink, but to calm my anxiety in case I couldn't get to a shop, like late on a Sunday. Even coming up with an excuse to get to the shops was hard normally, so under these circumstances would be awful. Now, with the lack of food, especially alcohol in my local supermarket, I know I would have been overly anxious.

On top of my worry about getting enough wine to drink, I would have also not been as present as I am at the moment, I wouldn't be as clear headed and able to listen to the news, and the events in the world. I'd most likely be making excuses to drink earlier in the day, because we are at home, or the weather is nice or it feels like a holiday, or we don't have to get up for work... I'm sure I would have been able to think of something that seemed like a good enough reason, but all it would have done would be to numb my feelings, to stop the worries, rather than deal with them. It wouldn't have fixed anything. I wouldn't have been so open to listening to events unfold. I would have been falling asleep in the evenings, or not remembering what happened the night before. I know this is true, because I know what I was like.

It might seem tempting to drink, to stop all the worry and to 'relax', especially at a time like this. I even found myself scrolling through Instagram recently and saw a photo of a glass of freshly poured wine next to the bottle. It was to reward someone for something they had achieved earlier in the day. Before I even realised, I had stopped scrolling and was just looking at it, remembering. And then I caught myself as I tend to do and I scrolled on by. I don't actually want to drink anymore, it's just that sometimes the memory is still there although now I know honestly that it won't help in the long run. It doesn't make things better.

I suppose what surprised me was how that feeling of remembering a 'nice' drink is still there, even after all this time, and even when I really don't want to drink. It catches me out. I'm not writing this because I'm worried or concerned I'll drink again, I honestly don't think I would. However, I do think it's good to address that those feelings are occasionally still there. I want to talk about it to let anyone reading this know that they aren't alone in those thoughts, and it's okay. Just because you remember, does not mean you have to relapse. Memories are going to take time to fade, it doesn't mean you have to give in to your demons, whatever they may be and it doesn't mean you are weak.

For me sunny relaxed late afternoons and evenings in the garden often used to mean having a glass or two of wine. (I'm being modest, we all know it never stopped there.) We have a big gas barbecue outside and we like to cook and eat outdoors whenever the weather is nice enough. (By we I mean I like to watch my husband cook). We were fortunate enough to have some lovely sunny and warm weather at the beginning of our first Covid-19 lockdown, and wanting to make these strange times as good as we could, we spent a lot of time outside with the kids. I built dens with Stanley, and he rode his bike around. Barn played with the dog and Katie moved from the sofa to the grass with her phone. Joe even came out to sit with us. It was lovely to make the most of it, and enjoy it, but at the same time, I was surprised at how many old feelings it brought up. It was only later as we spoke about dinner that I had that feeling of wanting a glass of wine. I suddenly felt like that would be the thing to complete the evening and as normal, as soon as I'd shifted that thought it was followed by a bit of sadness that I wouldn't be able to experience that again. The sadness never lasts for long now, it's just a fleeting thing, but it is annoying.

I never thought I would be able to say that I'm not worried by the idea of never drinking again, but I can. Even saying that though, I am surprised how there are still little things that set me off. I don't miss drinking, but sometimes, I miss that feeling of being the same as other people. I have a lovely time without it though. It doesn't change anything really, it certainly doesn't make me any more fun, or make an evening any better. In fact I know now, without a shadow of a doubt that I am a better person without it, so I guess that is why I'm so surprised when I get that little bit of envy. Our minds are funny old things, aren't they? I mean to remain wired so strongly for something for such a long time.

I read an interesting article from The Independent, called "Let's try 'Dry Covid- ' lockdown is the time to kick our national alcohol habit for good." I've often struggled with the advertising and easy availability of alcohol in our country. It's one of the reasons I think I struggled both to identify my drinking problem, but also to do anything about it. Seeing so many other people enjoy a drink and use alcohol for such a variety of reasons, like socialising or relaxing, it is easy to think it is a normal thing to do. It's everywhere, from adverts to soap operas, and normally only the fun, positive side of things is portrayed. They forget to show us the hangovers, stupid mistakes and embarrassments that occur when you drink heavily, unless of course they are depicting a dramatic story and usually then it is over pretty quickly once they've moved on to the next storyline. Once you're on the slippery slope you can struggle to see the blurry line between what a 'normal' drinker is and what a 'problem' drinker is. If you're like I was, you'll also look for any excuse available to make yourself feel normal.

Once you've identified that problem and you choose to do something about it, you find your perspective changing. While you might not change yourself, your outlook certainly will. For someone who relied on alcohol on a daily basis for many years, once I removed it from my life, I had this great big gap that needed filling. I needed to relearn a lot of things, from talking to people to how I behaved in certain situations. It was much harder than I thought it would be. In the background is the little voice that tells you that you are missing out if you don't drink, that everyone else drinks, that it is normal to drink and so much fun, and to be honest, what else will you do with your time? I really struggled with that and the reinforcement from advertising made it harder. It's why I relapsed and why it took me three 'proper' attempts to get sober. I don't count all the times I talked about stopping drinking but didn't really follow through on my plan. I felt abnormal from the minute I stopped drinking and I hated feeling like that. I thought people would notice, like I had a neon sign above my head making me stand out from the crowd. I didn't know how to ''be' anymore, and I didn't like not fitting in. Fitting in was something I had wanted to do for most of my life and yet here I was choosing to be different. I didn't know how to socialise, and didn't want to, but more importantly because most of the drinking I had done had been at home, I didn't know how to be at home either. I couldn't relax and I couldn't focus for a long time. If I had gone through this lockdown when I was drinking, I would have been unbearable. There is no way I could have bought enough wine to have lasted me, even for one week I would have needed over fourteen bottles. I would have been visiting the shops every day, and I would have had to class that as essential travel for me, I would have been ill without it. I am so thankful that I am not like that anymore. The author of that article stated that sales of alcohol during the crisis so far have risen by 50%, a figure I had previously heard on the news. While I suppose some of it can be justified, for example, if we are unable to go to restaurants, it is likely that some of the expense is due to food and drink being purchased at home to replace what would have been eaten out. It is also possible that some has been bought in bulk in order to stock pile for the future, and therefore sales may even out as people are able to get back to normal, however long that may take. The writer cites the World Health Organisation saying that they advise that drinking should not be used as a coping mechanism throughout this time. I would argue that we shouldn't be using it as a coping mechanism at any time, but that is probably the benefit of hindsight talking. I wonder whether now perhaps would be a good time to try going without, to slow down and take the time to abstain? I've read other articles that suggest lockdown isn't so different from the early days of recovery so it might be a good time to start? For me I always found that despite my good thoughts and efforts, it was near impossible to not stop at a shop on the way home for a few bottles if I didn't have much at home. I would tell myself I didn't need it, or that I could have a night off, but for a very long time it was too hard to do without. Not being able to shop removes one argument, although I know it would have been very difficult for me, and probably made me quite bad tempered. On the other hand, for much of my early recovery, in fact, for most of the first three years of my sobriety I did go into social hibernation. I didn't want to go out and look different, or feel different, or be questioned, the list was endless really, so it was easier to stay at home. Our current lockdown provides much the same basis, but without the need to make excuses to anyone. It's just a chance to batten down the hatches and recover, without having to make any explanations other than the ones we want to.

Of course, like I did, many people will probably question whether they even have a problem. There are so many people posting pictures and memes of people drinking, you know the sort of thing, like a mum giving her kids juice boxes and then having a wine box to herself, or the one about needing to stockpile wine, or 'funnier' still is the one about needing AA and a dietician when lockdown is over. Well they all seem funny, until they aren't. I'd have laughed at some of them once, but now I feel a bit sad when I see them now. I don't want to drink my way through life, numbing the good along with the bad. Sometimes things are tough, but do you know what? The good is better when you are present to remember it, and sobriety is so worth the effort. In response to all the 'funny' posts, I'd say this. If you can't do a few weeks in lockdown without drinking then maybe, just maybe you should have a closer look. Maybe noticing it now could be the opportunity to stop something before it runs away with you?

The peace and quiet in my head since I've been taking my anti-anxiety medicine is something that I love. For the first time in a very long time I've not got a constant chatter in my head... but... I worry that it's going to affect my creativity. At least for the first couple of weeks it seemed harder to write. Maybe that has something to do with lockdown too, there isn't so much to write about if I can't go out is there? In the last couple of weeks things are slowly coming back to normal which is a relief. At least at home it is, outside lockdown is still going strong so there is only so much normality we can achieve. I wondered whether my ability to write was just down to my crazy mind, and now I'm getting a handle on the crazy, I wondered if I'd lost the creative side.
I was very concerned about taking medication. I thought it might change me. I spent so long drinking wine, and changing my character in that way, that now I am as keen as possible to not do anything that affects my mood or feelings. It's nice to just be me without worrying if something is making me different, but I can't deny, this time it makes a welcome change. I still feel like me, just calmer, quieter, and considering how I was, that is only a good thing.

I was supposed to be seeing the doctor a few after starting my medication for a review as it is 'acute', they need to check it's okay and agreeing with me. Luckily it seems to be, because I haven't got a hope of getting in there at the moment! I phoned before the lockdown and asked if they would like to give my appointment to someone else that needs it and just give me a repeat prescription, under the circumstances. I thought they might put their foot down and make me keep the appointment but to my surprise, I was told that they had already cancelled my appointment, although no-one had told me! This was right back before the lockdown, but when things were beginning to get worse. I managed eventually to get a repeat prescription, and then tried to get into our pharmacy, which I hadn't appreciated had reduced its hours to 10-12 and then 2-4pm. So I couldn't get in, as I was on my way to work and began to stress out that I would run out. It isn't ideal when your anti-anxiety medication begins to make you anxious! My daughter offered to go for me and was there with plenty of time before the 12pm closure, but due to the social distancing measures in place she ended up in a queue outside. She waited and told me at 12pm they closed the doors turning the last three people in the queue away. Bless her, would you believe she stood there and waited for two hours for them to open again rather than leave and come back later? She didn't want the queue to get too big again and she didn't complain once, but did tell me she wished she had taken her earphones so she had something to do while she waited!

It's not all positive though. I was reading on one of my online groups recently about a comment from another member who was devastated by the comments of someone from her AA group. In a similar situation to my own, she had attended the group and told the others that she was feeling better, now that her medication was working, she went on to tell them that she had been sober for the longest time, and was expecting support and encouragement from the group. Instead someone stood up, and retorted that she wasn't sober if she was relying on medication. It hit her in a weak spot and she said that she almost immediately relapsed, wondering what the point was. Although from the outside I don't agree that she can blame this other person for her relapse, I do know how it feels to be judged or criticised, and to feel like you aren't understood. I felt so sorry for this person, that she had got so far, and was unable to ignore the comments of this person, who really shouldn't have felt the need to comment on her progress in such a way. It made me feel terrible for her, but I'm not sure that I agree that, he made her drink again, like she claimed. Ultimately the only person that has the responsibility for our drinking is ourselves.

I guess for anyone with a bit of an addictive personality, there is always going to be a worry that one dependence will turn into another. No-one wants to rely on anything really, and I know from experience that having relied on alcohol, and overcome it, I don't want to ever be back in that place again.

In hindsight I don't think medication affects my sobriety, but I also think it is a slippery slope for anyone, especially those who have had a dependency. I think, I, like anyone else, need to be aware of what I take, but ultimately, I think we need to do whatever it is that we need to help us overcome our individual problems. Those looking in from the outside will never quite understand, because they don't experience things as we do. We are all different and so, we all need different things to help us through, but we need to do it without the judgement of others, like the man from the AA group. His opinions weren't helpful or needed, and it makes me wonder what his insecurities are for him to speak to someone else that way.

Looking back, it seems odd that I could turn so many things into a reason to be able to drink, but then that's what our society does as a whole really isn't it? Everywhere you look there is an advert or a program, something condoning the use of alcohol as a reward, as a commiseration, as a celebration, to drown your sorrows, to have fun, to relax you, to give you courage, the list goes on and on. I've always looked forward to the holidays. If you rewind a few years it was always because a holiday meant another reason it was 'okay' to drink. Holidays meant relaxation, and no work, even if we didn't go away anywhere. It was nice to be able to turn the alarm clocks off for a few days, and not worry about getting up early. To pour a glass of wine just that little bit earlier, especially in the summer, because that was what people do, or have a couple of extras. To drink socially, or to relax at home in the sunshine with that nice cold drink.

I think a large part of drinking starts as a way to relax, but also as a way to fit in. We want to connect, to be with like-minded people and drinking allows us to join the club and be part of 'it'. I'm not really sure what 'it' is, I just knew that I didn't want to miss out. It was nice to join my friends in a beer garden on a night out, it was fun to chat on the phone with a friend, sharing a bottle even if we weren't together, but now, I'm not sure that these relationships were that genuine. I mean, how could they be when the 'me' that was there wasn't me, but an intoxicated version? As time went on though, these moments weren't enough, and when others went home, so did I, but I'd open another bottle when I got there.

Even now I sometimes romanticise the idea of drinking although it is getting much rarer. I can get a little lost in my memories, and those I have conjured up that aren't real, like the idea of sitting somewhere enjoying a glass of something. A few months ago I was outside a restaurant and looking in through the window I saw a family sitting down to eat. It sounds like I am a stalker, I'm not, I had a valid reason for being there. It was about 4.30pm and at first glance I saw them with their sparkling water and I was impressed, it reassured me that I wasn't the only one not to drink. But then, much to my disappointment, the waiter bought them over a beer and a bottle of wine. That's when the envy crept in. It really annoys me that it's still there, that I am envious over something that I don't even actually want anymore, but it sparked the whole conversation in my head wishing I could drink 'normally'. I mean what even is a normal drink? I can take a step back now, whereas a few years ago, I wouldn't have been able to. I can look at it, and think, "Yeah okay, they want a drink. I don't need one." Normally my thoughts are followed up with relief that I don't need something to take the edge off anymore, that I am able to just be me, whether it suits others or not. Sometimes, I even feel a little bit of pity, that others need a substance to help them have a good time.

Something in our culture needs to change. I think it is slowly, but alcohol is so ingrained, it isn't going to happen over-night. When I was growing up in the 1980's it was common for cigarette adverts to be everywhere, on the TV and in football stadiums particularly. Something changed, someone somewhere realised that smoking might do more harm than good and gradually people cracked down on the advertising. I hope one day the same happens with alcohol. People can decide whether they want to drink or not without it being rammed down their throats. We don't need actresses on adverts telling us that Bailey's makes Christmas special, and we don't need soap operas normalising daily drinking. For people that can take it or leave it so to speak, it is fine, but for people like me, and there are so many of us out there, we don't need reasons to excuse our drinking or to increase it, because that is what we do. At least it is until we stop. After that we look for reasons to see our behaviour as normal, but without the alcohol, and messages reinforcing how good it is really don't help. So nowadays, I still look forward to holidays and any other special occasion but it's no longer an excuse to drink. Instead it's a time to be present and enjoy myself, knowing I am being a genuine version of myself, that I can claim full responsibility for what I say and do and that'll I remember everything. It's not a bad place to be!

Something else that helps me a great deal is practicing gratitude. It sounds like such an easy thing to do, but in the same way, it is so easy to forget to do it. Back at the beginning of my recovery I read somewhere about having a gratitude practice, about at the end of the day thinking and appreciating everything good you have. I try to do it each night. I have so much to be grateful for, so I like to acknowledge it. I try to notice it at other times too, I think the more you try to notice, the more you see, and the more you appreciate what you have. I guess it's about changing your perceptions. For example, a few weeks ago I was driving to work when my little boy saw an aeroplane flying overhead in the distance. He was excited and shouted out to me, "Mummy!

Airplane!" I asked him if he thought it was taking people on holiday. It was such a throwaway comment, one I have made many times before, well, that or asking him if he thought it was going to the moon. But of course, things are a little different at the moment because of the coronavirus. There can't be many people going on holiday at the moment, in fact, it's more likely that those who are away, are worrying about how to get back. I feel terribly sad for all of those who are affected, don't get me wrong, but actually surprisingly it helps make me realise what I have and feel incredibly grateful for that. I told you that we'd never taken the kids abroad before, so managed to take them away to Corfu in 2018. It was lovely, and in 2019 we decided to go to Spain for a week. We had two holidays in two years with Thomas Cook, and literally a week or ten days after we got back the company went into administration. I know a lot of people weren't so lucky and lost their holidays. We don't get to go on many holidays like that, so to have two that we could enjoy safely was amazing, and I am so appreciative that we could enjoy both the holidays before the company had trouble.

It's easy to see all the negativity in the world, especially when we are struggling with other things. There is a lot to worry about to be honest, but I try to look for the good where I can. Over the years trying to have faith that things will work out in the way they are meant to has been one of the things that has kept me going. When things get rough, I try to remember that there is a bigger picture, that things are sent to try us and although times may be hard, on the whole, they work themselves out in the long run. I once read something that said, if you won't remember the worry in five years, don't spend five minutes on it now. Or something along those lines anyway.

In the same vein, I learned that my next two half marathons, the Tavy 13 and Plymouth were postponed because of the virus. Quite frankly I was relieved as it took the decision away from me. I didn't have to worry about missing out, because no one will be running it, and while it was disappointing, I am glad that the organisers were being proactive. I'm grateful that it's one less thing I had to think about. I know that so many people are disappointed that their races and other events are being cancelled, and I know that it's frustrating when so much time and effort has gone into training, but there will be other races. I'm not sure when, but there will. But, it got me thinking… I was so disappointed that I didn't get a place in the London Marathon Ballot. Equally, I was disappointed that I didn't get a place in the London Landmarks Half. That was what prompted me to book a place on The Vitality Big Half that I ran back in March in London. The thing is, if I hadn't been disappointed about missing out, then I wouldn't have booked that one, and enjoyed running it. And if I had got a place in either of the other two, then I wouldn't have been able to run them anyway, as they were both postponed. So actually, looking on the positive side, I think I'm pretty lucky. Things worked out quite well for me on this occasion.

It's easy to focus on the negative, or if not focus on it, then just see that side of things more easily than the positive. It's just about changing the way we look at things. I'm even trying to apply it to work. Working with my family can be tricky, but it has its positives. I have a lot of flexibility. I can take my son to work when it suits me and he loves riding his bike around in the compound outside when we shut the gates and he is safe. Over the New Year, we moved into a new premises. We'd outgrown our old building and were lucky enough to secure a new one, which was literally opposite our old one. Our new building took some work to get to where we wanted it to be, but was a blank canvas that could be designed to how we wanted it. At one point though we found there was a leak in the roof. It wasn't a major deal, but it was something that we didn't need at an already busy and costly time. However, rather than focusing on the leak, I actually managed to feel grateful for it. The reason I did was because it happened before we got all of our machinery and equipment into place. If it had happened then, and leaked onto that or our materials then it would have cost us a fortune. There is often a silver lining, even when we least expect them.

Probably one of the most challenging things is dealing with other people. I really had to toughen up and get a thicker skin, because I think only those in our sober tribe and those supporting us closely will really understand us. Only recently I had another comment from the another family member. She followed my Instagram account and then criticised my post, which I found strange. We had always been fairly close, and I know she had experiences of addiction in her family, with her late father particularly, so I do feel she should have known better or been kinder at least. I don't expect everyone to be sober, or to want to be, because not everyone has a drinking problem. Personally, I do have a problem. And, I'm not the only one. I found getting to where I am now really hard, and although I no longer feel like I am missing out, sometimes the memory of drinking is still there, and I don't like to trigger it. It isn't that I am jealous of those who drink, I just don't really like being reminded of the past. I don't want to see it being joked about as I know how hard it was to get sober. I don't care so much what everyone else shares, but actually, I do find it triggering/upsetting/offensive to see posts glamourising what is effectively a poison to me in my newsfeed. In the same way, I don't like adverts or comments on TV either. I can't limit everything I see, but I can have a voice about it. Sharing my thoughts helps me, and talking to others in a similar situation makes me feel understood and validated in my feelings.

The thing is, regardless of the words I write, no one knows what is in my head. You can read everything I have ever written and know that I am generally positive about my sobriety, but you won't necessarily know that somedays I still have little wobbles. This one day I had a wobble that caught me off guard. Lee phoned to say he was going to stay at work late, and the first thought into my mind, while he was still on the phone was to think, "I'll just pour some wine then." It caught me off guard because I haven't had a spontaneous thought like that in a long time. It really isn't that I am longing for it, it's just that I drank for such a long time that it feels a bit ingrained really.

It's the same with the comment from this woman. I like that people follow me, and read what I've written, I'm glad if it helps. I also understand if you don't, and not everyone will agree with me all the time either. I don't want it to seem like I am preaching, because that really isn't my intention, but it is important for me to voice my feelings, as I know connection helps us to overcome our difficulties, and I know that I am not the only person out there who was in my situation. I want people to be able to see that there is a way to be happy without alcohol in their lives, if that is what they are looking for. It made me upset to have someone tell me how I should feel, that apparently it should be okay for posts full of alcohol and jokes about it to fill my newsfeed because it will make me stronger, if I can't drink 'responsibly'. It's hard for people who haven't been there to understand quite what a fight those of us with addictions have, but that comment hit a sore point. What does it actually mean to drink responsibly? My first thoughts were that this person perhaps had already had a few drinks and so wasn't thinking about what they were saying, followed by the fact that perhaps they are sensitive about the amount they drink themselves? If I were being judgemental it would perhaps be correct because a lot of her frequent posts involve wine, but I'm only guessing.

Whatever the reason for the comment, I am sick of having drinking glamourised. We don't need it. It's nice for those who want it, but we shouldn't be justifying it to get through the day or a tricky time. While it can be explained away as saying it's 'fun' actually we need to remember that it's an addictive drug. Would the reaction be the same if we posted jokes about doing a line of cocaine in the evenings? Would that still be so 'funny'? Maybe I'm being too harsh? I just find it frustrating and hurtful to be told what I should think or feel by someone who hasn't been there and therefore can't understand.

I don't always get it right, and the anxious person I am, I worry that I've upset people, but I'm sure not everyone feels the same when they message me. Ultimately these are my thoughts, and my experiences, and while I don't want to offend, I will keep posting my opinion because that's what it is about. My writing is genuine. The things I write about are things I've experienced. The words are my own and the photos are real, unlike some websites which are full of purchased stock images.

Letting go is often easier said than done, well at least it is for me. I've often wondered why I remember things so well, especially the things that I'd rather forget, it's not intentional. It's not even like I'm holding a grudge, because often, it's not just other people I remember things about, it's myself too. Sometimes the thoughts will come out of nowhere and I'll suddenly be caught in a spin remembering something I said years ago, and I mean literally years ago. I doubt anyone else would even remember, and yet, there I am beating myself up about it. I doubt I can be the only one, although when I mention it, many people tell me I just need to let things go, to forget about it.

I've often said, we can't change the past, so there's no point in regretting the things that have got us to the point we are at now. My mistakes have gained me my sobriety and for that I will be eternally grateful, but of course, that doesn't mean I am proud of everything in my past. I'm not sure anyone could say they were proud of everything though?

Mistakes in many ways shape who we are. We grow and we learn and we can't always get everything right. We are human after all. I suppose the most important thing is that we learn from our mistakes. That we try not to repeat them and actually use our experiences for good, rather than continually reminding ourselves what failures we are, because largely we aren't, even when we make mistakes. Most of us are trying to do the best we can, and we have to remember that. In that way, reflecting on our mistakes is no bad thing, if it helps remind us what we have learned and what not to do moving forwards, but that doesn't mean we should let ourselves become overwhelmed with what we should not have done.

Sometimes we can't fix past mistakes, sometimes things are set in stone, or forgotten even, with others moving on. Sometimes however we can fix things. We can face up to our mistakes and try to make situations better. I'm not saying it's easy. In fact sometimes it is anything but easy. It can be terrifying to own up to something, to admit something you aren't proud of, and yet, when you have dealt with it, it relieves a weight from your shoulders that you possibly didn't even know you were carrying. Guilt and memories are funny like that. We think we've packed them away, we think we have moved on, and that they are safer left in their boxes, but sometimes, opening and unpacking those things, and confronting them, makes us feel so much better in the long run.

It takes time. I couldn't have dealt with facing up to everything at once. Nor could I have listed everything I wanted to deal with, but actually over time thoughts unearth themselves. Four years into my sobriety I still get confronted with random thoughts from out of the blue, but now I decide what to do with them, whether I want to confront them, or whether actually they are silly memories that I need to let go. That's important too. We mustn't feel that we have to deal with every little thing, because everyone makes mistakes or says something wrong, or at the wrong time. It doesn't make us bad. We aren't bad people.

I try to remember that no matter what, I can't change the past, I can't go back, and do you know what? I wouldn't want to. I'm a firm believer in thinking everything happens for a reason. The things I've done helped me become who I am, and I can't assume that's just the good things. It's all the things, good, bad and indifferent. We need to remember that, and be kind to ourselves, not just the bits we like, but all of who we are as individuals. We should let people in, let them care about us, forgive us, and be kind. Being hard on ourselves is difficult for those around us too. It can be wearing for those who care about us if we are always down on ourselves. Even when we don't mean to be.

Life throws us challenges, as long as we continue doing the best we can, it's all we can do, and sometimes, we need to accept that is enough.

CHAPTER 16
2021

There is no end to my story. I'm still here and I'm still trying and for that I am immensely grateful. It could have been very different for me and for my family. I am so lucky to have them. It's taken far more hard work that I would have liked to reinvent myself without alcohol in my life, but do you know what, it is so worth it and I am glad I won the battle in the end.

Thank you for reading my journey, and good luck on yours. I have one last thing to share with you, a poem I found right back at the beginning of my recovery. It's only short, but resonates deeply with me. It's called Autobiography in Five Short Chapters and it is by Portia Nelson, I hope you like it.

Autobiography in Five Short Chapters

By Portia Nelson

Chapter One

I walk down the street.

There is a deep hole in the sidewalk.

I fall in.

I am lost.... I am helpless.

It isn't my fault.

It takes forever to find a way out.

Chapter Two

I walk down the same street.

There is a deep hole in the sidewalk.

I pretend I don't see it.

I fall in again.

I can't believe I am in this same place.

But, it isn't my fault.

It still takes a long time to get out.

Chapter Three

I walk down the same street.

There is a deep hole in the sidewalk.

I see it is there.

I still fall in... it's a habit... but,

my eyes are open.

I know where I am.

It is my fault.

I get out immediately.

Chapter Four

I walk down the same street.

There is a deep hole in the sidewalk.

I walk around it.

Chapter Five

I walk down another street.

A LITTLE BIT OF HELPFUL ADVICE...

Getting sober is not easy, I'd love to say it is and all you have to do is stop drinking, but I don't want to lie. It is so good to be sober, so in the long run it is worth it and there are things you can do to help yourself. Here's a few ideas.

- Awareness. It sounds rubbish, but by being aware of what you are drinking you no longer have your head in the sand. This is one of the first things that made me realise just how much I was drinking. I didn't change it for a while, mainly because I wasn't ready to, but just realising how bad I was made me want to change something.

- Measure your units. They say that men and women in the UK shouldn't exceed 14 units of alcohol a week, but of course that does not take into consideration your weight or height, which must play a part. The guidelines state that one unit is 76ml of wine. Well I know for sure that my glass was 250ml at the very least and it wasn't the biggest. So I was drinking 3 units per glass, and at least six glasses a night, which means I was drinking more than the weekly guidelines per day. Every single day. Easy to run away with you isn't it? Especially when you think it's only a glass or two. Glasses at home are the worst, they are so big compared to measures in the pub, so just be aware.

- Drink free days. It's easier said than done for some people, I know I really struggled with this. It made me stress out because I was so dependent on wine for my anxiety, and if I didn't drink one night, which was rare, I just thought about when I could

196

drink again. I'm all or nothing when it comes to drinking. Cutting down though is best, so try to manage two days at least a week if you can.

- Stay in contact. Meetings work for some people, but if you don't want to meet other people, like me, you can try online communities. There are so many out there, and knowing you are not alone can really help.

- Ask for help. I for one am not keen on doctors, but, there is a time and a place, and for me, I needed some advice from a medical professional. I drank too much to be able to go cold turkey without it being dangerous. Please don't try to stop suddenly if you are in a similar place, as it can cause a lot of problems for your body.

- Find things to do. Everyone has triggers that are individual to them. For me it was certain situations or times of the day. I found 5-6pm particularly hard, and associated it with my first glass of the evening, it's sometimes called 'wine o'clock' for that reason. If I could get out and get past that time, it was often easier not to have a drink. Although don't get me wrong, I still found it hard. New hobbies and time for yourself help, so don't be afraid to spoil yourself a little.

- Expect it to be hard. I read a lot of experiences from people who maybe did a few days without drinking and then seemed fixed. Don't get me wrong, it is amazing if that works for you, but don't be disheartened if it doesn't. I almost felt there was something wrong with me, (besides addiction), when I wasn't fixed straight away. It is a hard road, but one I wouldn't change, I just think it might have been easier for me if I had been prepared for it to be so hard.

- Don't feel you have to explain yourself or make excuses. Frankly it is no-one else's business whether you drink or don't drink. Don't put yourself into situations where you are challenged to the point of breaking your resolve and don't feel you need to tell others anything. It is up to you what you do, and I found a lot of people don't understand. It took a while for me to be okay with my new found sobriety and be able to take judgements from others without it affecting me. Now I feel stronger in my sobriety, it makes no difference to me what other people think, but it's taken a long time to feel like that. I still worry I'll be judged, but I am wrong more often than not, and it's just because I don't like being different!
- Save your money. A lot of people find putting the money you would spend on drinking into a jar, and visually being able to see how much you have saved yourself is really helpful. There are apps which do this for you too!
- Remember that no one is the same. Different approaches work for different people. Just because something does or doesn't work for you doesn't mean it is wrong. Just do what you need to, and remember that it will get easier. I promise. It just takes time.

So here are a few tips to help you stay sober, if you're struggling, because the last thing anyone needs is to relapse.

- Occupy yourself, keep your mind busy and it will help you to stay positive. Take advantage of the extra time you might have on your hands to take up a new hobby.
- If you're not already a member of any online groups, join some. Your online sober community can provide a safe place to talk to

many people in similar situations and share, even if you can't or don't want to meet up.

- Get outside if you can. I went for a run this morning and spent the afternoon in the garden with the kids. I felt so much better. Granted, this is easier when the weather is nice, but make the most of it, when it is and take advantage of it where we can. Walking, running and fresh air are all good for your mental well-being, and can really help. A walk in the rain can be equally as refreshing!
- Distance yourself from negativity, whether it's social media or excessive news consumption, don't get too drawn in, and make sure that your news comes from a trustworthy source.
- Whether you are home alone, or with others, try to stay in contact with others, especially those who understand you. Isolation feeds addiction so don't do it!
- Equally, remember the difference your contact will make on others, don't isolate them either. It's easy to forget how others can feel when they want to help you.
- Remember, you can drink, you just choose not to!

Other people's attitudes and actions have been one of the hardest things to cope with, one of the biggest things to rock the boat so to speak. It's not just when people say the wrong thing, it's actually probably worse when they don't say anything at all.

Here's my little list of pointers for dealing with friends who are alcohol free.

- Please offer me a drink. Just because I don't drink alcohol anymore, doesn't mean I am no longer thirsty.
- Don't assume what I want to do. Ask me.

- Don't assume what I can do or can't do. Ask me.
- Don't talk about me with other friends. I already feel like I'm the object of everyone's interests so please don't make it worse.
- If I've told you about my problem, respect that, and keep my trust.
- Invite me out, and let me make the decision of whether I want to go or not.
- Put up with me changing my mind too. Sometimes what I want to do will seem like a good idea and then I'll realise that I'm not ready. Or that I just don't want to do it anymore.
- Don't try to offer me advice unless you've been there.
- Don't make judgements for me.
- Understand that I'll find some days better than others and I might not always understand why, so I might not being very good at explaining it.

This list is by no means definitive, and only based on my personal circumstances, but I think they might be useful. So let me know what you think and if there's anything else you'd add to it.

ABOUT THE AUTHOR

Claire Hatwell is a wife, a Mum of four and an advocate for sober living having fought a battle with addiction and won.

She writes the popular blog My Not So Secret Diary and can be found online at
https://www.facebook.com/ClairesSecretDiary
or on her website
https://www.soberme.co.uk

Her range of sobriety cards and gifts are available here
https://www.etsy.com/uk/shop/SoberMe

Printed in Great Britain
by Amazon

68179027R00121